GOD AND THE STATE

MICHAEL BAKUNIN

GOD AND THE STATE

WITH A NEW INTRODUCTION AND
INDEX OF PERSONS by **PAUL AVRICH**
PROFESSOR OF HISTORY, QUEENS COLLEGE

DOVER PUBLICATIONS, INC., NEW YORK

Published in Canada by General Publishing Company, Ltd.,
30 Lesmill Road, Don Mills, Toronto, Ontario.
Published in the United Kingdom by Constable and Company, Ltd.,
10 Orange Street, London WC 2.

This Dover edition, first published in 1970, is an
unabridged and unaltered republication of the edition published in 1916 by Mother Earth Publishing
Association, New York. A new Introduction and
Index of Persons, prepared by Paul Avrich, have
been added.

International Standard Book Number: 0-486-22483-X
Library of Congress Catalog Card Number: 75-105664

Manufactured in the United States of America
Dover Publications, Inc.
180 Varick Street
New York, N.Y. 10014

INTRODUCTION TO THE DOVER EDITION

This man was born not under an ordinary star but under a comet.
—ALEXANDER HERZEN

It was nearly a century ago that Michael Bakunin wrote what was to become his most celebrated pamphlet, *God and the State*. At that time, anarchism was emerging as a major force within the revolutionary movement, and the name of Bakunin, its foremost champion and prophet, was as well known among the workers and radical intellectuals of Europe as that of Karl Marx, with whom he was competing for leadership of the First International.

In contrast to Marx, Bakunin had won his reputation chiefly as an activist rather than a theorist of rebellion. He was born into the Russian landed gentry in 1814, but as a young man abandoned his army commission and noble heritage for a career as a professional revolutionist. Leaving Russia in 1840, at the age of twenty-six, he dedicated his life to a struggle against tyranny in all its forms. He was not one to sit in libraries, studying and writing about predetermined revolutions. Impatient for action, he threw himself into the uprisings of 1848 with irrepressible exuberance, a Promethean figure moving with the tide of revolt from Paris to the barricades of Austria and Germany. Men like Bakunin, a companion remarked, "grow in a hurricane and ripen better in stormy weather than in sunshine."[1] But his arrest during the Dresden insurrection of 1849 cut short his feverish revolutionary activity. He spent the next eight years in prison, six of them in the darkest dungeons of tsarist Russia, and when he emerged, his sentence commuted to a life term of Siberian exile, he was toothless from scurvy and his health seriously impaired. In 1861, however, he escaped his warders and embarked upon a sensational odyssey that encircled the globe and made his name a legend and an object of worship in radical groups all over Europe.

As a romantic rebel and an active force in history, Bakunin exerted a personal attraction that Marx could never rival. "Everything about him was colossal," recalled the composer Richard Wagner, a fellow participant in the Dresden uprising, "and he was full of a primitive

---

[1] E. Lampert, *Studies in Rebellion* (London, 1957), p. 118.

exuberance and strength."[2] Bakunin's "love for the fantastic, for unusual, unheard-of adventures, which open up vast horizons, the end of which cannot be foreseen," to quote his own words, inspired extravagant dreams in others, and by the time of his death in 1876 he had won a unique place among the adventurers and martyrs of the revolutionary tradition. His broad magnanimity and childlike enthusiasm, his burning passion for liberty and equality, his volcanic onslaughts against privilege and injustice—all this gave him enormous human appeal in the libertarian circles of his day.

But Bakunin, as his critics never tired of pointing out, was not a systematic thinker. Nor did he ever claim to be. For he considered himself a revolutionist of the deed, "not a philosopher and not an inventor of systems, like Marx."[3] He refused to recognize the existence of any preconceived or preordained laws of history. He rejected the view that social change depends upon the gradual unfolding of "objective" historical conditions. He believed, on the contrary, that men shape their own destinies, that their lives cannot be squeezed into a Procrustean bed of abstract sociological formulas. "No theory, no ready-made system, no book that has ever been written will save the world," Bakunin declared. "I cleave to no system, I am a true seeker."[4] By teaching the workers theories, he said, Marx would only succeed in stifling the revolutionary fervor every man already possesses—"the impulse to liberty, the passion for equality, the holy instinct of revolt." Unlike Marx's "scientific" socialism, his own socialism, Bakunin asserted, was "purely instinctive."[5]

Bakunin's influence, then, as Peter Kropotkin remarked, was primarily that of a "moral personality" rather than of an intellectual authority. Although he wrote prodigiously, he did not leave a single finished book to posterity. He was forever starting new works which, owing to his turbulent existence, were broken off in mid-course and never completed. His literary output, in Thomas Masaryk's description, was a "patchwork of fragments." And yet, however erratic and unmethodical, his writings abound in flashes of insight that illuminate some of the most important social questions of his time—and of ours.

[2] E. H. Carr, *Michael Bakunin* (New York, 1961), p. 196.
[3] Iu. M. Steklov, *Mikhail Aleksandrovich Bakunin*, 4 vols. (Moscow, 1926–1927), III, 112.
[4] Carr, *Michael Bakunin*, p. 175.
[5] M. A. Bakunin, *Oeuvres*, 6 vols. (Paris, 1895–1913), II, 399; Steklov, *Mikhail Aleksandrovich Bakunin*, I, 189.

God and the State is an excellent case in point. It is disjointed, repetitious, poorly organized, and full of digressions and long footnotes that tend to soften its polemical impact. All the same, it is forceful and energetic, and packed with arresting aphorisms that testify to Bakunin's remarkable intuitive gifts. As a result, *God and the State* has become the most widely read and frequently quoted of all Bakunin's works. But perhaps the main reason for its popularity is that, in vivid language and relatively brief compass, it sets forth the basic elements of Bakunin's anarchist creed.

The keynote of *God and the State* is Bakunin's repudiation of authority and coercion in every form. In a withering passage he vents his fury on "all the tormentors, all the oppressors, and all the exploiters of humanity—priests, monarchs, statesmen, soldiers, public and private financiers, officials of all sorts, policemen, gendarmes, jailers and executioners, monopolists, economists, politicians of all shades, down to the smallest vendor of sweetmeats." But the leading institutions of man's enslavement—"my two *bêtes noires*," he calls them—are the church and the state. Every state has been an instrument by which a privileged few have wielded power over the immense majority. And every church has been a loyal ally of the state in the subjugation of mankind. Governments throughout history have used religion both as a means of keeping men in ignorance and as a "safety-valve" for human misery and frustration. More than that, the very essence of religion is the disparagement of humanity for the greater glory of God. "God being everything," Bakunin writes, "the real world and men are nothing; God being truth, justice, goodness, beauty, power, and life, man is falsehood, inequity, evil, ugliness, impotence, and death. God being master, man is the slave." No less than the state, then, religion is the negation of freedom and equality. Thus if God really exists, Bakunin concludes, inverting a famous dictum of Voltaire's, "it would be necessary to abolish him."

Bakunin proclaimed an all-out war against the church and the state. If men are to be free, they must throw off the double yoke of spiritual and temporal authority. To accomplish this they must bring to bear the two "most precious qualities" with which they are endowed: the power to think and the desire to rebel. Human history itself began with an act of thought and rebellion. If Adam and Eve had obeyed the Almighty when he forbade them to touch the tree of knowledge, humanity would have been condemned to perpetual bondage. But Satan—"the eternal rebel, the first freethinker and the emancipator of worlds"—persuaded them to taste the fruit of knowledge and liberty. These same weapons—reason and rebellion—must now be turned against the church and the state. And once they are overthrown there will dawn a new Eden for mankind, a new era of freedom and happiness.

But the task of liberation, warns Bakunin, will not be easy. For already a new class has emerged that aims to keep the masses in ignorance in order to rule over them. These would-be oppressors are the intellectuals, above all Marx and his followers, "priests of science" ordained in a new privileged church of superior education. The rule of the intellectuals, according to Bakunin, would be no less oppressive than the rule of kings or priests or holders of property. The government of an educated elite, like the worst religious and political despotisms of the past, "cannot fail to be impotent, ridiculous, inhuman, cruel, oppressive, exploiting, maleficent."

With this warning Bakunin anticipated the "new class" label that later critics were to pin on Marx's heirs in the twentieth century. He assailed the theorists and system-builders whose so-called "science of society" was sacrificing real life on the altar of scholastic abstractions. He refused to shed the fictions of religion and metaphysics merely to see them replaced by what he considered the new fictions of pseudo-scientific sociology. He therefore proclaimed a "revolt of life against science, or rather, against the government of science." For the true mission of science and learning, he insisted, was not to govern men but to rescue them from superstition, drudgery, and disease. "In a word," he writes in *God and the State*, "science is the compass of life but not life itself." But how can this new form of despotism be avoided? Bakunin's answer was to wrest education from the monopoly grasp of the privileged classes and make it available equally to everyone. Like capital, learning must cease to be the patrimony of the few and become the patrimony of all men, "in order that the masses, ceasing to be flocks led and shorn by privileged priests, may take into their own hands the direction of their destinies."

Such was the powerful message of *God and the State*. But it did not appear in print until 1882, six years after Bakunin's death. For it was only then that the manuscript was discovered among his papers by two well-known anarchists, Carlo Cafiero and Elisée Reclus, who had been closely associated with him during the last years of his life, when his libertarian doctrines saw their fullest flowering. The manuscript breaks off in mid-sentence, and Cafiero and Reclus, as they relate in their Preface, believing it to be part of a letter or report, undertook to search for the remainder. But their efforts were in vain, and they brought out the truncated text as a pamphlet in Geneva, having given it the title of *Dieu et l'état* (God and the State) by which it was to become famous. They did not suspect—nor were they ever to learn—that the manuscript was actually an unpublished segment of *The Knouto-Germanic Empire and the Social Revolution*, an ambitious work on which Bakunin had labored fitfully between 1870 and 1872 but had never managed to complete.

The Knouto-Germanic Empire—the title derives from the unholy alliance between Russian and German authoritarianism to stamp out social progress—is one of Bakunin's longest and most important literary efforts. He himself called it his "testament," and devoted considerable energy to its composition, ranging in characteristically discursive fashion over a wide assortment of subjects from history and politics to metaphysics and religion. Part I, written against the background of the Franco-Prussian War, deals mainly with the resistance by the French to German imperialism, and was published in pamphlet form in 1871. What Cafiero and Reclus called "God and the State" was a fragment from the unpublished and unfinished Part II, for which Bakunin's own title was "The Historical Sophisms of the Doctrinaire School of Communism," which, apart from being unwieldy, bears but little relation to its contents. The "God and the State" section was written, as we know from Bakunin's diary, in February and March of 1871, on the eve of the Paris Commune, but several of its themes—notably the idea that government and religion have always worked together to keep men in chains—can be traced to Bakunin's then unpublished essay, *Federalism, Socialism, and Antitheologism* (written in 1867), and were to crop up again in his polemics with Giuseppe Mazzini after the fall of the Commune in May 1871.

Within a short time after its initial publication by Cafiero and Reclus, *God and the State* became the most widely circulated of Bakunin's works, a distinction which, nearly a century later, it still enjoys. It has been translated into many languages, including English, German, Dutch, Italian, Spanish, Russian, Polish, Czech, Rumanian, and Yiddish. The first English translation, by the American anarchist Benjamin Tucker, appeared in Boston in 1883, scarcely a year after the original French edition. Tucker's rendering suffered, however, from a number of handicaps. Not only had Cafiero and Reclus altered Bakunin's text in a few places to give his French a smoother and more literary quality, but they had transposed several passages and occasionally misread Bakunin's handwriting, which was as chaotic as his other personal traits. When the first correct French text was published in 1908, it was followed by a new English edition, which appeared in London in 1910. This was essentially the Tucker translation, revised to conform to Bakunin's actual text, that is, without the alterations of Cafiero and Reclus. Still another edition, of which the present volume is a reprint, was brought out by Emma Goldman's Mother Earth press in 1916, and is identical with the London version except for a few minor differences in wording and punctuation.

While the *God and the State* segment first appeared in 1882, it was not for another generation that the full text of *The Knouto-Germanic Empire*—Parts I and II, together with two additional fragments and the remainder of a long footnote—saw its way into print. It finally appeared in the six-volume French edition of Bakunin's collected works (1895–1913), edited by the leading anarchist historian Max Nettlau (Volume I) and by James Guillaume (Volumes II-VI), Bakunin's faithful Swiss disciple. The whole of Part II of *The Knouto-Germanic Empire* occupies pages 9-177 of the third volume, of which pages 18-131 contain the correct text of what Cafiero and Reclus had published under the title of *God and the State*. Pages 9-17 are prefatory remarks of little consequence, while the remainder (pages 132-177) is a continuation of an attack by Bakunin on the French liberal philosopher Victor Cousin (1792–1867) that begins on the final page of *God and the State*. Cousin was the founder of the "eclectic school" and, as the name implies, had drawn on a wide variety of theories in what Bakunin regarded as a misguided attempt to prove the existence of God and to justify the existence of the state.

The continuation of *God and the State* consists of thirteen numbered paragraphs, peppered with critical asides and footnotes, in which Cousin's doctrines are summarized and refuted. Paragraph thirteen breaks off in mid-sentence, and no conclusion has been found. Near the end, however, there is the beginning of a footnote which also breaks off in mid-sentence but the remainder of which was discovered by Max Nettlau and published (it runs to some sixty pages) in the first volume of Bakunin's collected works. Unfortunately, Nettlau headed the note "God and the State," thereby adding to the confusion, for when subsequent writers refer to "God and the State" it is sometimes hard to tell whether they mean Nettlau's footnote or the famous essay of the same name.

Nettlau apparently chose the title because the footnote elaborates upon a passage from *God and the State*, in which Rousseau is denounced as "a prophet of the doctrinaire state" and "the real creator of modern reaction." Resuming the attack, Bakunin rejects Rousseau's notion of social contract—by which men surrender part of their liberty to the state in exchange for security and harmony—as a shameless fiction and a subterfuge for tyranny. He refuses to accept even the smallest limitation of human liberty. "Every enslavement of men," he writes, "is at the same time a limit on my own freedom." "I am a free man only so far as I recognize the humanity and liberty of all men around me. In respecting their humanity, I respect my own." The social contract, moreover, while recognizing the individual and the state, overlooks society, which for Bakunin is the "natural mode of existence of people living together."[6]

Apart from the continuation of *God and the State* and the footnote on Rousseau, there are yet two more segments of *The Knouto-Germanic Empire* which did not appear in print till long after Bakunin's death. The first of these is a loosely constructed "Appendix" with the grandiloquent title of "Philosophical Considerations on the Divine Phantom, on the Real World, and on Man." Written in the autumn of 1870, it is divided into five sections: System of the World; Man: Intelligence, Will; Animality, Humanity; Religion; Philosophy, Science.[7] The second, called "An Essay Against Marx," was drafted in November and December of 1872, shortly after the Hague Congress of the First International, at which the controversy between Marx and Bakunin reached a dramatic climax with the latter's expulsion from the organization. It is hardly surprising, therefore, that Marx should be the villain of the

---

[6] *Oeuvres*, I, 264-326. The whole of *The Knouto-Germanic Empire*, Part II, including *God and the State*, the continuation on Cousin, and the long footnote are conveniently brought together in a single volume of the Russian edition of Bakunin's collected works: *Izbrannye sochineniia* (Petrograd, 1922), II, 123-264.

[7] *Oeuvres*, III, 179-405. For a summary with extracts in English, see K. J. Kenafick, *Michael Bakunin and Karl Marx* (Melbourne, 1948), pp. 331ff.

piece. Bakunin assails him as "the dictator of the International," and compares his worship of the state and centralized authority with that of his fellow German, Bismarck. Marx, he says, impelled by his Teutonic urge to dominate, has forgotten his own stirring words from the program of the International: "The emancipation of the workers must be the task of the workers themselves."[8]

When Bakunin wrote this final segment of *The Knouto-Germanic Empire*, he had less than four years to live. But for generations to come his disciples continued to proclaim his anarchist message and to shower abuse upon the proponents of "scientific socialism." Again and again they warned that political power is evil, that it corrupts all who wield it, that government of any kind stifles the revolutionary spirit of the people and robs them of their freedom. Like Bakunin before them, they called for the overthrow of the church and the state, from whose ruins they foresaw the emergence of a Golden Age of justice and equality, a shining era of freedom in which men would direct their own affairs without interference from any authority.

PAUL AVRICH

New York
January, 1970

---

[8] *Oeuvres*, IV, 397-510; *Archives Bakounine* (Leiden, 1965), II, 169-219.

SUGGESTIONS FOR FURTHER READING

The standard biography in English is *Michael Bakunin* by E. H. Carr, London, 1937, Vintage paperback, 1961. A clear exposition of Bakunin's philosophy is Eugene Pyziur's *The Doctrine of Anarchism of Michael A. Bakunin*. Milwaukee, 1955. Another useful study is K. J. Kenafick, *Michael Bakunin and Karl Marx*, Melbourne, 1948. In addition, several works in English contain valuable chapters on Bakunin, notably Max Nomad, *Apostles of Revolution*, Boston, 1939, Collier paperback, 1961; Franco Venturi, *Roots of Revolution*, New York, 1960, Universal paperback, 1967; Richard Hare, *Portraits of Russian Personalities Between Reform and Revolution*, London, 1959; E. Lampert, *Studies in Rebellion*, London, 1957; Edmund Wilson, *To the Finland Station*, New York, 1940, Anchor paperback, 1953; G. D. H. Cole, *Socialist Thought: Marxism and Anarchism, 1850–1890*, London, 1954; and Alexander Gray, *The Socialist Tradition*, London, 1946, Harper paperback, 1968. See also George Woodcock, *Anarchism*, Cleveland, Meridian paperback, 1962; James Joll, *The Anarchists*, London, 1964, Universal paperback, 1966; Paul Avrich, *The Russian Anarchists*, Princeton, 1967; and Isaiah Berlin, "Herzen and Bakunin on Individual Liberty," in *Continuity and Change in Russian and Soviet Thought*, ed. E. J. Simmons, Cambridge, Mass., 1955. Finally, for a selection of Bakunin's writings in English translation, see G. P. Maximoff, ed., *The Political Philosophy of Bakunin*, New York, 1953, Free Press paperback, 1964.

"If God really existed it would be necessary to abolish him."

PREFACE TO FIRST FRENCH EDITION

One of us is soon to tell in all its details the story of the life of Michael Bakunin, but its general features are already sufficiently familiar. Friends and enemies know that this man was great in thought, will, persistent energy; they know also with what lofty contempt he looked down upon wealth, rank, glory, all the wretched ambitions which most human beings are base enough to entertain. A Russian gentleman related by marriage to the highest nobility of the empire, he was one of the first to enter that intrepid society of rebels who were able to release themselves from traditions, prejudices, race and class interests, and set their own comfort at naught. With them he fought the stern battle of life, aggravated by imprisonment, exile, all the dangers and all the sorrows that men of self-sacrifice have to undergo during their tormented existence.

A simple stone and a name mark the spot in the cemetery of Berne where was laid the body of Bakunin. Even that is perhaps too much to honor the memory of a worker who held vanities of that sort in such slight esteem. His friends surely will raise to him no ostentatious tombstone or statue. They know with what a huge laugh he would have received them, had they spoken to him of a commemorative structure erected to his glory; they knew, too, that the true way to honor their dead is to continue their work—with the same ardor and perseverance that they themselves brought to it. In this case, indeed, a difficult task demanding all our efforts, for among the revolutionists of the present generation not one has labored more fervently in the common cause of the Revolution.

In Russia among the students, in Germany among the insurgents of Dresden, in Siberia among his brothers in exile, in America, in England, in France, in Switzerland, in Italy, among all earnest men, his direct influence has been considerable. The originality of his ideas, the imagery and vehemence of his eloquence, his untiring zeal in propagandism, helped too by the natural majesty of his person and by a powerful vitality, gave Bakunin access to all the revolutionary groups, and his efforts left deep traces everywhere, even upon those who, after having welcomed him, thrust him out because of a difference of object or method. His correspondence was most extensive; he passed entire nights in preparing long letters to his friends in the revolutionary world, and some of these letters, written to strengthen the timid, arouse the sluggish, and outline plans of propagandism or revolt, took on the proportions of veritable volumes. These letters more than anything else explain the prodigious work of Bakunin in the revolutionary movement of the century. The pamphlets published by him, in Russian, French, and Italian, however important they may be, and however useful they may have been in spreading the new ideas, are the smallest part of Bakunin's work.

The present memoir, "God and the State," is really a fragment of a letter or report. Composed in the same manner as most of Bakunin's other writings, it has the same literary fault, lack of proportion; moreover it breaks off abruptly: we have searched in vain to discover the end of the manuscript. Bakunin never had the time necessary to finish all the tasks he undertook. One work was not completed when others were already under way. "My life itself is a fragment," he said to those who criticised his writings. Nevertheless, the readers of "God and the State" certainly will not regret that Bakunin's memoir, incomplete though it be, has been published. The questions discussed in it are treated decisively and with a singular vigor of logic. Rightly addressing himself only to his honest opponents, Bakunin demonstrates to them the emptiness of their belief in that divine authority on which all temporal authorities are founded; he proves to them the purely human genesis of all governments; finally, without stopping to discuss those bases of the State already condemned by public morality, such as physical superiority, violence, nobility, wealth, he does justice to the theory which would entrust science with the government of societies. Supposing even that it were possible to recognize, amid the conflict of rival ambitions and intrigues, who are the pretenders and who are the real savants, and that a method of election could be found which would not fail to lodge the power in the hands of those whose knowledge is authentic, what guarantee could they offer us of the wisdom and honesty of their government? On the contrary, can we not foresee in these new masters the same follies and the same crimes found in those of former days and of the present time? In the first place, science is not: it is becoming. The learned man of to-day is but the know-nothing of to-morrow. Let him once imagine that he has reached the end, and for that very reason he sinks beneath even the babe just born. But, could he recognize truth in its essence, he can only corrupt himself by privilege and corrupt others by power. To establish his government, he must try, like all chiefs of State, to arrest the life of the masses moving below him, keep them in ignorance in order to preserve quiet, and gradually debase them that he may rule them from a loftier throne.

For the rest, since the *doctrinaires* made their appearance, the true or pretended "genius" has been trying his hand at wielding the sceptre of the world, and we know what it has cost us. We have seen them at work, all these savants: the more hardened the more they have studied; the narrower in their viwes the more time they have spent in examining some isolated fact in all its aspects; without any experience of life, because they have long known no other horizon than the walls of their cheese; childish in their passions and vanities, because they have been unable to participate in serious struggles and have never learned the true proportion of things. Have we not recently witnessed the foundation of a whole school of "thinkers"—wretched courtiers, too, and people of unclean lives—who have constructed a whole cosmogony for their sole use? According to them, worlds have been created, societies have developed, revolutions have overturned nations, empires have gone down in blood, poverty, disease, and death have been the queens of humanity, only to raise up an *élite* of academicians, the full-blown flower, of which all other men are but the manure. That these editors of the *Temps* and the *Debats* may have leisure to "think," nations live and die in ignorance; all other human beings are destined for death in order that these gentlemen may become immortal!

But we may reassure ourselves: all these academicians will not have the audacity of Alexander in cutting with his sword the Gordian knot; they will not lift the blade of Charlemagne. Government by science is becoming as impossible as that of divine right, wealth, or brute force. All powers are henceforth to be submitted to pitiless criticism. Men in whom the sentiment of equality is born suffer themselves no longer to be governed; they learn to govern themselves. In precipitating from the heights of the heavens him from whom all power is reputed to descend, societies unseat also all those who reigned in his name. Such is the revolution now in progress. States are breaking up to give place to a new order, in which, as Bakunin was fond of saying, "human justice will be substituted for divine justice." If it is allowable to cite any one name from those of the revolutionists who have taken part in this immense work of renovation, there is not one that may be singled out with more justice than that of Michael Bakunin.

Carlo Cafiero.
Elisée Reclus.

GOD AND THE STATE

HO are right, the idealists or the materialists?
The question once stated in this way' hesitation
becomes impossible. Undoubtedly the idealists
are wrong and the materialists right. Yes, facts
are before ideas; yes, the ideal, as Proudhon
said, is but a flower, whose root lies in the material conditions of existence. Yes, the whole
history of humanity, intellectual and moral, political and social, is but a reflection of its economic history.

All branches of modern science, of true and disinterested science, concur in proclaiming this grand truth, fundamental and decisive: The social world, properly speaking,
the human world—in short, humanity—is nothing other than
the last and supreme development—at least on our planet
and as far as we know—the highest manifestation of animality. But as every development necessarily implies a
negation, that of its base or point of departure, humanity is
at the same time and essentially the deliberate and gradual
negation of the animal element in man; and it is precisely
this negation, as rational as it is natural, and rational only
because natural—at once historical and logical, as inevitable
as the development and realization of all the natural laws
in the world—that constitutes and creates the ideal, the
world of intellectual and moral convictions, ideas.

Yes, our first ancestors, our Adams and our Eves, were,
if not gorillas, very near relatives of gorillas, omnivorous,
intelligent and ferocious beasts, endowed in a higher degree
than the animals of any other species with two precious
faculties—*the power to think* and *the desire to rebel*.

These faculties, combining their progressive action in

history, represent the essential factor, the negative power in the positive development of human animality, and create consequently all that constitutes humanity in man.

The Bible, which is a very interesting and here and there very profound book when considered as one of the oldest surviving manifestations of human wisdom and fancy, expresses this truth very naively in its myth of original sin. Jehovah, who of all the good gods adored by men was certainly the most jealous, the most vain, the most ferocious, the most unjust, the most bloodthirsty, the most despotic, and the most hostile to human dignity and liberty—Jehovah had just created Adam and Eve, to satisfy we know not what caprice; no doubt to while away his time, which must weigh heavy on his hands in his eternal egoistic solitude, or that he might have some new slaves. He generously placed at their disposal the whole earth, with all its fruits and animals, and set but a single limit to this complete enjoyment. He expressly forbade them from touching the fruit of the tree of knowledge. He wished, therefore, that man, destitute of all understanding of himself, should remain an eternal beast, ever on all-fours before the eternal God, his creator and his master. But here steps in Satan, the eternal rebel, the first freethinker and the emancipator of worlds. He makes man ashamed of his bestial ignorance and obedience; he emancipates him, stamps upon his brow the seal of liberty and humanity, in urging him to disobey and eat of the fruit of knowledge.

We know what followed. The good God, whose foresight, which is one of the divine faculties, should have warned him of what would happen, flew into a terrible and ridiculous rage; he cursed Satan, man, and the world created by himself, striking himself so to speak in his own creation, as children do when they get angry; and, not content with smiting our ancestors themselves, he cursed them in all the generations to come, innocent of the crime committed by their forefathers. Our Catholic and Protestant theologians look upon that as very profound and very just, precisely because it is monstrously iniquitous and absurd. Then, remembering that he was not only a God of vengeance and wrath, but also a God of love, after having tormented the existence of a few milliards of poor human beings and condemned them to an eternal hell, he took pity on the rest, and, to save them and reconcile his eternal and divine love with his eternal and divine anger, always greedy for victims and blood, he sent into the world, as an expiatory victim, his only son, that he might be killed by men. That is called the mystery of the Redemption, the basis of all the Christian religions. Still, if the divine Savior had saved the human world! But no; in the paradise promised by Christ, as we know, such being the formal announcement, the elect will number very few. The rest, the immense majority of the generations present and to come, will burn eternally in hell. In the meantime, to console us, God, ever just, ever good, hands over the earth to the government of the Napoleon Thirds, of the William Firsts, of the Ferdinands of Austria, and of the Alexanders of all the Russias.

Such are the absurd tales that are told and the monstrous doctrines that are taught, in the full light of the nineteenth century, in all the public schools of Europe, at the express command of the government. They call this civilizing the people! Is it not plain that all these governments are systematic poisoners, interested stupefiers of the masses?

I have wandered from my subject, because anger gets hold of me whenever I think of the base and criminal means which they employ to keep the nations in perpetual slavery, undoubtedly that they may be the better able to fleece them. Of what consequence are the crimes of all the Tropmanns in the world compared with this crime of treason against humanity committed daily, in broad day, over the whole surface of the civilized world, by those who dare to call themselves the guardians and the fathers of the people? I return to the myth of original sin.

God admitted that Satan was right; he recognized that

the devil did not deceive Adam and Eve in promising them knowledge and liberty as a reward for the act of disobedience which he had induced them to commit; for, immediately they had eaten of the forbidden fruit, God himself said (see Bible): "Behold, the man is become as one of the gods, to know good and evil; prevent him, therefore, from eating of the fruit of eternal life, lest he become immortal like Ourselves."

Let us disregard now the fabulous portion of this myth and consider its true meaning, which is very clear. Man has emancipated himself; he has separated himself from animality and constituted himself a man; he has begun his distinctively human history and development by an act of disobedience and science—that is, by *rebellion* and by *thought*.

Three elements or, if you like, three fundamental principles constitute the essential conditions of all human development, collective or individual, in history: (1) *human animality;* (2) *thought;* and (3) *rebellion*. To the first properly corresponds *social and private economy;* to the second, *science;* to the third, *liberty*.

Idealists of all schools, aristocrats and *bourgeois,* theologians and metaphysicians, politicians and moralists, religionists, philosophers, or poets, not forgetting the liberal economists—unbounded worshippers of the ideal, as we know—are much offended when told that man, with his magnificent intelligence, his sublime ideas, and his boundless aspirations, is, like all else existing in the world, nothing but matter, only a product of *vile matter*.

We may answer that the matter of which materialists speak, matter spontaneously and eternally mobile, active, productive, matter chemically or organically determined and manifested by the properties or forces, mechanical, physical, animal, and intelligent, which necessarily belong to it—that this matter has nothing in common with the *vile matter* of the idealists. The latter, a product of their false abstraction, is indeed a stupid, inanimate, immobile thing, incapable of giving birth to the smallest product, a *caput mortuum,* an *ugly* fancy in contrast to the *beautiful* fancy which they call *God;* as the opposite of this supreme being, matter, their matter, stripped by them of all that constitutes its real nature, necessarily represents supreme nothingness. They have taken away from matter intelligence, life, all its determining qualities, active relations or forces, motion itself, without which matter would not even have weight, leaving it nothing but impenetrability and absolute immobility in space; they have attributed all these natural forces, properties, and manifestations to the imaginary being created by their abstract fancy; then, interchanging *rôles,* they have called this product of their imagination, this phantom, this God who is nothing, "supreme Being," and, as a necessary consequence, have declared that the real being, matter, the world, is nothing. After which they gravely tell us that this matter is incapable of producing anything, not even of setting itself in motion, and consequently must have been created by their God.

At the end of this book I exposed the fallacies and truly revolting absurdities to which one is inevitably led by this imagination of a God, let him be considered as a personal being, the creator and organizer of worlds; or even as impersonal, a kind of divine soul spread over the whole universe and constituting thus its eternal principle; or let him be an idea, infinite and divine, always present and active in the world, and always manifested by the totality of material and definite beings. Here I shall deal with one point only.

The gradual development of the material world, as well as of organic animal life and of the historically progressive intelligence of man, individually or socially, is perfectly conceivable. It is a wholly natural movement from the simple to the complex, from the lower to the higher, from the inferior to the superior; a movement in conformity with all our daily experiences, and consequently in conformity also with our natural logic, with the distinctive laws of our mind, which being formed and developed only by the aid of these same experiences, is, so to speak, but the mental, cerebral reproduction or reflected summary thereof.

The system of the idealists is quite the contrary of this. It is the reversal of all human experiences and of that universal and common good sense which is the essential condition of all human understanding, and which, in rising from the simple and unanimously recognized truth that twice two are four to the sublimest and most complex scientific considerations—admitting, moreover, nothing that has not stood the severest tests of experience or observation of things and facts—becomes the only serious basis of human knowledge.

Very far from pursuing the natural order from the lower to the higher, from the inferior to the superior, and from the relatively simple to the more complex; instead of wisely and rationally accompanying the progressive and real movement from the world called inorganic to the world organic, vegetables, animal, and then distinctively human—from chemical matter or chemical being to living matter or living being, and from living being to thinking being—the idealists, obsessed, blinded, and pushed on by the divine phantom which they have inherited from theology, take precisely the opposite course. They go from the higher to the lower, from the superior to the inferior, from the complex to the simple. They begin with God, either as a person or as divine substance or idea, and the first step that they take is a terrible fall from the sublime heights of the eternal ideal into the mire of the material world; from absolute perfection into absolute imperfection; from thought to being, or rather, from supreme being to nothing. When, how, and why the divine being, eternal, infinite, absolutely perfect, probably weary of himself, decided upon this desperate *salto mortale* is something which no idealist, no theologian, no metaphysician, no poet, has ever been able to understand himself or explain to the profane. All religions, past and present, and all the systems of transcendental philosophy hinge on this unique and iniquitous mystery.*   Holy men, inspired lawgivers, prophets, messiahs, have searched it for life, and found only torment and death. Like the ancient sphinx, it has devoured them, because they could not explain it. Great philosophers, from Heraclitus and Plato down to Descartes, Spinoza, Leibnitz, Kant, Fichte, Schelling, and Hegel, not to mention the Indian philosophers, have written heaps of volumes and built systems as ingenious as sublime, in which they have said by the way many beautiful and grand things and discovered immortal truths, but they have left this mystery, the principal object of their transcendental investigations, as unfathomable as before. The gigantic efforts of the most wonderful geniuses that the world has known, and who, one after another, for at least thirty centuries, have undertaken anew this labor of Sisyphus, have resulted only in rendering this mystery still more incomprehensible. Is it to be hoped that it will be unveiled to us by the routine speculations of some pedantic disciple of an artificially warmed-over metaphysics at a time when all living and serious spirits have abandoned that ambiguous science born of a compromise—historically explicable no doubt—between the unreason of faith and sound scientific reason?

It is evident that this terrible mystery is inexplicable—that is, absurd, because only the absurd admits of no explanation. It is evident that whoever finds it essential to his happiness and life must renounce his reason, and return, if he can, to naive, blind, stupid faith, to repeat with Tertullianus and all sincere believers these words, which sum up the very quintessence of theology: *Credo quia absurdum.* Then all discussion ceases, and nothing remains but the triumphant stupidity of faith. But immediately there

---

*I call it "iniquitous" because, as I believe I have proved in the Appendix alluded to, this mystery has been and still continues to be the consecration of all the horrors which have been and are being committed in the world; I call it unique, because all the other theological and metaphysical absurdities which debase the human mind are but its necessary consequences.

arises another question: *How comes an intelligent and well-informed man ever to feel the need of believing in this mystery?*

Nothing is more natural than that the belief in God, the creator, regulator, judge, master, curser, savior, and benefactor of the world, should still prevail among the people, especially in the rural districts, where it is more widespread than among the proletariat of the cities. The people, unfortunately, are still very ignorant, and are kept in ignorance by the systematic efforts of all the governments, who consider this ignorance, not without good reason, as one of the essential conditions of their own power. Weighted down by their daily labor, deprived of leisure, of intellectual intercourse, of reading, in short of all the means and a good portion of the stimulants that develop thought in men, the people generally accept religious traditions without criticism and in a lump. These traditions surround them from infancy in all the situations of life, and artificially sustained in their minds by a multitude of official poisoners of all sorts, priests and laymen, are transformed therein into a sort of mental and moral habit, too often more powerful even than their natural good sense.

There is another reason which explains and in some sort justifies the absurd beliefs of the people—namely, the wretched situation to which they find themselves fatally condemned by the economic organization of society in the most civilized countries of Europe. Reduced, intellectually and morally as well as materially, to the minimum of human existence, confined in their life like a prisoner in his prison, without horizon, without outlet, without even a future if we believe the economists, the people would have the singularly narrow souls and blunted instincts of the bourgeois if they did not feel a desire to escape; but of escape there are but three methods—two chimerical and a third real. The first two are the dram-shop and the church, debauchery of the body or debauchery of the mind; the third is social revolution. Hence I conclude this last will be much more potent than all the theological propagandism of the freethinkers to destroy to their last vestige the religious beliefs and dissolute habits of the people, beliefs and habits much more intimately connected than is generally supposed. In substituting for the at once illusory and brutal enjoyments of bodily and spiritual licentiousness the enjoyments, as refined as they are real, of humanity developed in each and all, the social revolution alone will have the power to close at the same time all the dram-shops and all the churches.

Till then the people, taken as a whole, will believe; and, if they have no reason to believe, they will have at least a right.

There is a class of people who, if they do not believe, must at least make a semblance of believing. This class, comprising all the tormentors, all the oppressors, and all the exploiters of humanity; priests, monarchs, statesmen, soldiers, public and private financiers, officials of all sorts, policemen, gendarmes, jailers and executioners, monopolists, capitalists, tax-leeches, contractors and landlords, lawyers, economists, politicians of all shades, down to the smallest vendor of sweetmeats, all will repeat in unison those words of Voltaire:

"If God did not exist, it would be necessary to invent him." For, you understand, "the people must have a religion." That is the safety-valve.

There exists, finally, a somewhat numerous class of honest but timid souls who, too intelligent to take the Christian dogmas seriously, reject them in detail, but have neither the courage nor the strength nor the necessary resolution to summarily renounce them altogether. They abandon to your criticism all the special absurdities of religion, they turn up their noses at all the miracles, but they cling desperately to the principal absurdity; the source of all the others, to the miracle that explains and justifies all the other miracles, the existence of God. Their God is not the vigorous and powerful being, the brutally positive God of theology. It is a nebulous, diaphanous, illusory being that vanishes into nothing at the first attempt to grasp it; it is a mirage, an *ignis fatuus* that neither warms nor illuminates. And yet they hold fast to it, and believe that, were it to disappear, all would disappear with it. They are uncertain, sickly souls, who have lost their reckoning in the present civilization, belonging to neither the present nor the future, pale phantoms eternally suspended between heaven and earth, and occupying exactly the same position between the politics of the bourgeois and the Socialism of the proletariat. They have neither the power nor the wish nor the determination to follow out their thought, and they waste their time and pains in constantly endeavoring to reconcile the irreconcilable. In public life these are known as bourgeois Socialists.

With them, or against them, discussion is out of the question. They are too puny.

But there are a few illustrious men of whom no one will dare to speak without respect, and whose vigorous health, strength of mind, and good intention no one will dream of calling in question. I need only cite the names of Mazzini, Michelet, Quinet, John Stuart Mill.* Generous and strong souls, great hearts, great minds, great writers, and the first the heroic and revolutionary regenerator of a great nation, they are all apostles of idealism and bitter despisers and adversaries of materialism, and consequently of Socialism also, in philosophy as well as in politics.

Against them, then, we must discuss this question.

First, let it be remarked that not one of the illustrious men I have just named nor any other idealistic thinker of

---

*Mr. Stuart Mill is perhaps the only one whose serious idealism may be fairly doubted, and that for two reasons: first, that, if not absolutely the disciple, he is a passionate admirer, an adherent of the positive philosophy of Auguste Comte, a philosophy which, in spite of its numerous reservations, is really Atheistic; second, that Mr. Stuart Mill is English, and in England to proclaim oneself an Atheist is to ostracise onself, even at this late day.

any consequence in our day has given any attention to the logical side of this question properly speaking. Not one has tried to settle philosophically the possibility of the divine *salto mortale* from the pure and eternal regions of spirit into the mire of the material world. Have they feared to approach this irreconcilable contradiction and despaired of solving it after the failures of the greatest geniuses of history, or have they looked upon it as already sufficiently well settled? That is their secret. The fact is that they have neglected the theoretical demonstration of the existence of a God, and have developed only its practical motives and consequences. They have treated it as a fact universally accepted, and, as such, no longer susceptible of any doubt whatever, for sole proof thereof limiting themselves to the establishment of the antiquity and this very universality of the belief in God.

This imposing unanimity, in the eyes of many illustrious men and writers to quote only the most famous of them who eloquently expressed· it, Joseph de Maistre and the great Italian patriot, Giuseppe Mazzini—is of more value than all the demonstrations of science; and if the reasoning of a small number of logical and even very powerful, but isolated, thinkers is against it, so much the worse, they say, for these thinkers and their logic, for universal consent, the general and primitive adoption of an idea, has always been considered the most triumphant testimony to its truth. The sentiment of the whole world, a conviction that is found and maintained always and everywhere, cannot be mistaken; it must have its root in a necessity absolutely inherent in the very nature of man. And since it has been established that all peoples, past and present, have believed and still believe in the existence of God, it is clear that those who have the misfortune to doubt it, whatever the logic that led them to this doubt, are abnormal exceptions, monsters.

Thus, then, the *antiquity* and *universality* of a belief should be regarded, contrary to all science and all logic, as sufficient and unimpeachable proof of its truth. Why?

Until the days of Copernicus and Galileo everybody believed that the sun revolved about the earth. Was not everybody mistaken? What is more ancient and more universal than slavery? Cannibalism perhaps. From the origin of historic society down to the present day there has been always and everywhere exploitation of the compulsory labor of the masses—slaves, serfs, or wage-workers—by some dominant minority; oppression of the people by the Church and by the State. Must it be concluded that this exploitation and this oppression are necessities absolutely inherent in the very existence of human society? These are examples which show that the argument of the champions of God proves nothing.

Nothing, in fact, is as universal or as ancient as the iniquitous and absurd; truth and justice, on the contrary, are the least universal, the youngest features in the development of human society. In this fact, too, lies the explanation of a constant historical phenomenon—namely, the persecution of which those who first proclaim the truth have been and continue to be the objects at the hands of the official, privileged, and interested representatives of "universal" and "ancient" beliefs, and often also at the hands of the same masses who, after having tortured them, always end by adopting their ideas and rendering them victorious.

To us materialists and Revolutionary Socialists, there is nothing astonishing or terrifying in this historical phenomenon. Strong in our conscience, in our love of truth at all hazards, in that passion for logic which of itself alone constitutes a great power and outside of which there is no thought; strong in our passion for justice and in our unshakable faith in the triumph of humanity over all theoretical and practical bestialities; strong, finally, in the mutual confidence and support given each other by the few who share our convictions—we resign ourselves to all the consequences of this historical phenomenon, in which we see the manifestation of a social law as natural, as necessary, and as invariable as all the other laws which govern the world.

This law is a logical, inevitable consequence of the *animal origin* of human society; for in face of all the scientific, physiological, psychological, and historical proofs accumulated at the present day, as well as in face of the exploits of the Germans conquering France, which now furnish so striking a demonstration thereof, it is no longer possible to really doubt this origin. But from the moment that this animal origin of man is accepted, all is explained. History then appears to us as the revolutionary negation, now slow, apathetic, sluggish, now passionate and powerful, of the past. It consists precisely in the progressive negation of the primitive animality of man by the development of his humanity. Man, a wild beast, cousin of the gorilla, has emerged from the profound darkness of animal instinct into the light of the mind, which explains in a wholly natural way all his past mistakes and partially consoles us for his present errors. He has gone out from animal slavery, and passing through divine slavery, a temporary condition between his animality and his humanity, he is now marching on to the conquest and realization of human liberty. Whence it results that the antiquity of a belief, of an idea, far from proving anything in its favor, ought, on the contrary, to lead us to suspect it. For behind us is our animality and before us our humanity; human light, the only thing that can warm and enlighten us, the only thing that can emancipate us, give us dignity, freedom, and happiness, and realize fraternity among us, is never at the beginning, but, relatively to the epoch in which we live, always at the end of history. Let us, then, never look back, let us look ever forward; for forward is our sunlight, forward our salvation. If it is justifiable, and even useful and necessary, to turn back to study our past, it is only in order to establish what we have been and what we must no longer be, what we have believed and thought and what we must no longer believe or think, what we have done and what we must do nevermore.

So much for *antiquity*. As for the *universality* of an error, it proves but one thing—the similarity, if not the perfect identity, of human nature in all ages and under all skies. And, since it is established that all peoples, at all periods of their life, have believed and still believe in God, we must simply conclude that the divine idea, an outcome of ourselves, is an error historically necessary in the development of humanity, and ask why and how it was produced in history and why an immense majority of the human race still accept it as a truth.

Until we shall account to ourselves for the manner in which the idea of a supernatural or divine world was developed and had to be developed in the historical evolution of the human conscience, all our scientific conviction of its absurdity will be in vain; until then we shall never succeed in destroying it in the opinion of the majority, because we shall never be able to attack it in the very depths of the human being where it had birth. Condemned to a fruitless struggle, without issue and without end, we should for ever have to content ourselves with fighting it solely on the surface, in its innumerable manifestations, whose absurdity will be scarcely beaten down by the blows of common sense before it will reappear in a new form no less nonsensical. While the root of all the absurdities that torment the world, belief in God, remains intact, it will never fail to bring forth new offspring. Thus, at the present time, in certain sections of the highest society, Spiritualism tends to establish itself upon the ruins of Christianity.

It is not only in the interest of the masses, it is in that of the health of our own minds, that we should strive to understand the historic genesis, the succession of causes which developed and produced the idea of God in the consciousness of men. In vain shall we call and believe ourselves Atheists, until we comprehend these causes, for, until then, we shall always suffer ourselves to be more or less governed by the clamors of this universal conscience whose secret we have not discovered; and, considering the natural weakness of even the strongest individual against the all-powerful influence of the social surroundings that trammel him, we are always in danger of relapsing sooner or later, in one way or another, into the abyss of religious absurdity. Examples of these shameful conversions are frequent in society to-day.

I have stated the chief practical reason of the power still exercised to-day over the masses by religious beliefs. These mystical tendencies do not signify in man so much an aberration of mind as a deep discontent at heart. They are the instinctive and passionate protest of the human being against the narrowness, the platitudes, the sorrows, and the shame of a wretched existence. For this malady, I have already said, there is but one remedy—Social Revolution.

In the meantime I have endeavored to show the causes responsible for the birth and historical development of religious hallucinations in the human conscience. Here it is my purpose to treat this question of the existence of a God, or of the divine origin of the world and of man, solely from the standpoint of its moral and social utility, and I shall say only a few words, to better explain my thought, regarding the theoretical grounds of this belief.

All religions, with their gods, their demigods, and their prophets, their messiahs and their saints, were created by the credulous fancy of men who had not attained the full development and full possession of their faculties. Consequently, the religious heaven is nothing but a mirage in which man, exalted by ignorance and faith, discovers his own image, but enlarged and reversed—that is, *divinized*. The history of religions, of the birth, grandeur, and decline of the gods who have succeeded one another in human belief, is nothing, therefore, but the development of the collective intelligence and conscience of mankind. As fast as they discovered, in the course of their historically progressive advance, either in themselves or in external nature, a power, a quality, or even any great defect whatever, they attributed them to their gods, after having exaggerated and enlarged them beyond measure, after the manner of children, by an act of their religious fancy. Thanks to this modesty and pious generosity of believing and credulous men, heaven has grown rich with the spoils of the earth, and, by a necessary consequence, the richer heaven became, the more wretched became humanity and the earth. God once installed, he was naturally proclaimed the cause, reason, arbiter, and absolute disposer of all things: the world thenceforth was nothing, God was all; and man, his real creator, after having unknowingly extracted him from the void, bowed down before him, worshipped him, and avowed himself his creature and his slave.

Christianity is precisely the religion *par excellence*, because it exhibits and manifests, to the fullest extent, the very nature and essence of every religious system, which is *the impoverishment, enslavement, and annihilation of humanity for the benefit of divinity.*

God being everything, the real world and man are nothing. God being truth, justice, goodness, beauty, power, and life, man is falsehood, iniquity, evil, ugliness, impotence, and death. God being master, man is the slave. Incapable of finding justice, truth, and eternal life by his own effort, he can attain them only through a divine revelation. But whoever says revelation says revealers, messiahs, prophets, priests, and legislators inspired by God himself; and these, once recognized as the representatives of divinity on earth, as the holy instructors of humanity, chosen by God himself to direct it in the path of salvation, necessarily exercise absolute power. All men owe them passive and unlimited obedience; for against the divine reason there is no human reason, and against the justice of God no terrestrial justice holds. Slaves of God, men must also be slaves of Church and State, *in so far as the State is consecrated by the Church.* This truth Christianity, better than all other religions that exist or have existed, understood, not excepting even the old Oriental religions, which included only distinct and privileged nations, while Christianity aspires to embrace entire humanity; and this truth Roman Catholicism,

alone among all the Christian sects, has proclaimed and
realized with rigorous logic. That is why Christianity is
the absolute religion, the final religion; why the Apostolic
and Roman Church is the only consistent, legitimate, and
divine church.

With all due respect, then, to the metaphysicians and religious idealists, philosophers, politicians, or poets: *The
idea of God implies the abdication of human reason and
justice; it is the most decisive negation of human liberty,
and necessarily ends in the enslavement of mankind, both
in theory and practice.*

Unless, then, we desire the enslavement and degradation
of mankind, as the Jesuits desire it, as the *mômiers,* pietists,
or Protestant Methodists desire it, we may not, must not
make the slightest concession either to the God of theology
or to the God of metaphysics. He who, in this mystical
alphabet, begins with A will inevitably end with Z; he who
desires to worship God must harbor no childish allusions
about the matter, but bravely renounce his liberty and humanity.

If God is, man is a slave; now, man can and must be
free; then, God does not exist.

I defy anyone whomsoever to avoid this circle; now,
therefore, let all choose.

Is it necessary to point out to what extent and in what
manner religions debase and corrupt the people? They destroy their reason, the principal instrument of human emancipation, and reduce them to imbecility, the essential condition of their slavery. They dishonor human labor, and make
it a sign and source of servitude. They kill the idea and
sentiment of human justice, ever tipping the balance to the
side of triumphant knaves, privileged objects of divine in-
dulgence. They kill human pride and dignity, protecting
only the cringing and humble. They stifle in the heart of
nations every feeling of human fraternity, filling it with
divine cruelty instead.

All religions are cruel, all founded on blood; for all

rest principally on the idea of sacrifice—that is, on the perpetual immolation of humanity to the insatiable vengeance of divinity. In this bloody mystery man is always the victim, and the priest—a man also, but a man privileged by grace—is the divine executioner. That explains why the priests of all religions, the best, the most humane, the gentlest, almost always have at the bottom of their hearts—and, if not in their hearts, in their imaginations, in their minds (and we know the fearful influence of either on the hearts of men)—something cruel and sanguinary.

None know all this better than our illustrious contemporary idealists. They are learned men, who know history by heart; and, as they are at the same time living men, great souls penetrated with a sincere and profound love for the welfare of humanity, they have cursed and branded all these misdeeds, all these crimes of religion with an eloquence unparalleled. They reject with indignation all solidarity with the God of positive religions and with his representatives, past, present, and on earth.

The God whom they adore, or whom they think they adore, is distinguished from the real gods of history precisely in this—that he is not at all a positive god, defined in any way whatever, theologically or even metaphysically. He is neither the supreme being of Robespierre and J. J. Rousseau, nor the pantheistic god of Spinoza, nor even the at once immanent, transcendental, and very equivocal god of Hegel. They take good care not to give him any positive definition whatever, feeling very strongly that any definition would subject him to the dissolving power of criticism. They will not say whether he is a personal or impersonal god, whether he created or did not create the world; they will not even speak of his divine providence. All that might compromise him. They content themselves with saying "God" and nothing more. But, then, what is their God? Not even an idea; it is an aspiration.

It is the generic name of all that seems grand, good, beautiful, noble, human to them. But why, then, do they

not say, "Man." Ah! because King William of Prussia and
Napoleon III. and all their compeers are likewise men:
which bothers them very much. Real humanity presents a
mixture of all that is most sublime and beautiful with all
that is vilest and most monstrous in the world. How do
they get over this? Why, they call one *divine* and the other
bestial, representing divinity and animality as two poles, between which they place humanity. They either will not or
cannot understand that these three terms are really but one,
and that to separate them is to destroy them.

They are not strong on logic, and one might say that
they despise it. That is what distinguishes them from the
pantheistical and deistical metaphysicians, and gives their
ideas the character of a practical idealism, drawing its inspiration much less from the severe development of a
thought than from the experiences, I might almost say the
emotions, historical and collective as well as individual, of
life. This gives their propaganda an appearance of wealth
and vital power, but an appearance only; for life itself becomes sterile when paralyzed by a logical contradiction.

This contradiction lies here: they wish God, and they
wish humanity. They persist in connecting two terms which,
once separated, can come together again only to destroy
each other. They say in a single breath: "God and the
liberty of man," "God and the dignity, justice, equality, fraternity, prosperity of men"—regardless of the fatal logic by
virtue of which, if God exists, all these things are condemned to non-existence. For, if God is, he is necessarily
the eternal, supreme, absolute master, and, if such a master
exists, man is a slave; now, if he is a slave, neither justice,
nor equality, nor fraternity, nor prosperity are possible for
him. In vain, flying in the face of good sense and all the
teachings of history, do they represent their God as ani-
mated by the tenderest love of human liberty: a master, whoever he may be and however liberal he may desire to show
himself, remains none the less always a master. His existence necessarily implies the slavery of all that is beneath

him. Therefore, if God existed, only in one way could he serve human liberty—by ceasing to exist.

A jealous lover of human liberty, and deeming it the absolute condition of all that we admire and respect in humanity, I reverse the phrase of Voltaire, and say that, *if God really existed, it would be necessary to abolish him.*

The severe logic that dictates these words is far too evident to require a development of this argument. And it seems to me impossible that the illustrious men, whose names so celebrated and so justly respected I have cited, should not have been struck by it themselves, and should not have perceived the contradiction in which they involve themselves in speaking of God and human liberty at once. To have disregarded it, they must have considered this inconsistency or logical license *practically* necessary to humanity's well-being.

Perhaps, too, while speaking of *liberty* as something very respectable and very dear in their eyes, they give the term a meaning quite different from the conception entertained by us, materialists and Revolutionary Socialists. Indeed, they never speak of it without immediately adding another word, *authority*—a word and a thing which we detest with all our heart.

What is authority? Is it the inevitable power of the natural laws which manifest themselves in the necessary concatenation and succession of phenomena in the physical and social worlds? Indeed, against these laws revolt is not only forbidden—it is even impossible. We may misunderstand them or not know them at all, but we cannot disobey them; because they constitute the basis and fundamental conditions of our existence; they envelop us, penetrate us, regulate all our movements, thoughts, and acts; even when we believe that we disobey them, we only show their omnipotence.

Yes, we are absolutely the slaves of these laws. But in such slavery there is no humiliation, or, rather, it is not slavery at all. For slavery supposes an external master, a legislator outside of him whom he commands, while these laws

are not outside of us; they are inherent in us; they constitute
our being, our whole being, physically, intellectually, and
morally: we live, we breathe, we act, we think, we wish only
through these laws. Without them we are nothing, *we are
not*. Whence, then, could we derive the power and the
wish to rebel against them?

In his relation to natural laws but one liberty is possible
to man—that of recognizing and applying them on an ever-
extending scale in conformity with the object of collective
and individual emancipation or humanization which he pur-
sues. These laws, once recognized, exercise an authority
which is never disputed by the mass of men. One must,
for instance, be at bottom either a fool or a theologian or
at least a metaphysician, jurist, or bourgeois economist to
rebel against the law by which twice two make four. One
must have faith to imagine that fire will not burn nor water
drown, except, indeed, recourse be had to some subterfuge
founded in its turn on some other natural law. But these
revolts, or, rather, these attempts at or foolish fancies of
an impossible revolt, are decidedly the exception; for, in general, it may be said that the mass of men, in their daily
lives, acknowledge the government of common sense—that
is, of the sum of the natural laws generally recognized—
in an almost absolute fashion.

The great misfortune is that a large number of natural
laws, already established as such by science, remain un-
known to the masses, thanks to the watchfulness of
these tutelary governments that exist, as we know, only
for the good of the people. There is another difficulty—
namely, that the major portion of the natural laws connected with the development of human society, which are
quite as necessary, invariable, fatal, as the laws that govern
the physical world, have not been duly established and recognized by science itself.

Once they shall have been recognized by science, and
then from science, by means of an extensive system of popular education and instruction, shall have passed into the

consciousness of all, the question of liberty will be entirely solved. The most stubborn authorities must admit that then there will be no need either of political organization or direction or legislation, three things which, whether they emanate from the will of the sovereign or from the vote of a parliament elected by universal suffrage, and even should they conform to the system of natural laws—which has never been the case and never will be the case—are always equally fatal and hostile to the liberty of the masses from the very fact that they impose upon them a system of external and therefore despotic laws.

The liberty of man consists solely in this: that he obeys natural laws because he has *himself* recognized them as such, and not because they have been externally imposed upon him by any extrinsic will whatever, divine or human, collective or individual.

Suppose a learned academy, composed of the most illustrious representatives of science; suppose this academy charged with legislation for and the organization of society, and that, inspired only by the purest love of truth, it frames none but laws in absolute harmony with the latest discoveries of science. Well, I maintain, for my part, that such legislation and such organization would be a monstrosity, and that for two reasons: first, that human science is always and necessarily imperfect, and that, comparing what it has discovered with what remains to be discovered, we may say that it is still in its cradle. So that were we to try to force the practical life of men, collective as well as individual, into strict and exclusive conformity with the latest data of science, we should condemn society as well as individuals to suffer martyrdom on a bed of Procrustes, which would soon end by dislocating and stifling them, life ever remaining an infinitely greater thing than science.

The second reason is this: a society which should obey legislation emanating from a scientific academy, not because it understood itself the rational character of this legislation (in which case the existence of the academy would become useless), but because this legislation, emanating from the academy, was imposed in the name of a science which it venerated without comprehending—such a society would be a society, not of men, but of brutes. It would be a second edition of those missions in Paraguay which submitted so long to the government of the Jesuits. It would surely and rapidly descend to the lowest stage of idiocy.

But there is still a third reason which would render such a government impossible—namely that a scientific academy invested with a sovereignty, so to speak, absolute, even if it were composed of the most illustrious men, would infalliby and soon end in its own moral and intellectual corruption. Even to-day, with the few privileges allowed them, such is the history of all academies. The greatest scientific genius, from the moment that he becomes an academician, an officially licensed *savant*, inevitably lapses into sluggishness. He loses his spontaneity, his revolutionary hardihood, and that troublesome and savage energy characteristic of the grandest geniuses, ever called to destroy old tottering worlds and lay the foundations of new. He undoubtedly gains in politeness, in utilitarian and practical wisdom, what he loses in power of thought. In a word, he becomes corrupted.

It is the characteristic of privilege and of every privileged position to kill the mind and heart of men. The privileged man, whether politically or economically, is a man depraved in mind and heart. That is a social law which admits of no exception, and is as applicable to entire nations as to classes, corporations, and individuals. It is the law of equality, the supreme condition of liberty and humanity. The principal object of this treatise is precisely to demonstrate this truth in all the manifestations of human life.

A scientific body to which had been confided the government of society would soon end by devoting itself no longer to science at all, but to quite another affair; and that affair, as in the case of all established powers, would be its own eternal perpetuation by rendering the society confided to its care ever more stupid and consequently more in need of its government and direction.

But that which is true of scientific academies is also true of all constituent and legislative assemblies, even those chosen by universal suffrage. In the latter case they may renew their composition, it is true, but this does not prevent the formation in a few years' time of a body of politicians, privileged in fact though not in law, who, devoting themselves exclusively to the direction of the public affairs of a country, finally form a sort of political aristocracy or oligarchy. Witness the United States of America and Switzerland.

Consequently, no external legislation and no authority— one, for that matter, being inseparable from the other, and both tending to the servitude of society and the degradation of the legislators themselves.

Does it follow that I reject all authority? Far from me such a thought. In the matter of boots, I refer to the authority of the bootmaker; concerning houses, canals, or railroads, I consult that of the architect or engineer. For such or such special knowledge I apply to such or such a *savant*. But I allow neither the bootmaker nor the architect nor the *savant* to impose his authority upon me. I listen to them freely and with all the respect merited by their intelligence, their character, their knowledge, reserving always my incontestable right of criticism and censure. I do not content myself with consulting a single authority in any special branch; I consult several; I compare their opinions, and choose that which seems to me the soundest. But I recognize no infallible authority, even in special questions; consequently, whatever respect I may have for the honesty and the sincerity of such or such an individual, I have no absolute faith in any person. Such a faith would be fatal to my reason, to my liberty, and even to the success of my undertakings; it would immediately transform me into a stupid slave, an instrument of the will and interests of others.

If I bow before the authority of the specialists and avow my readiness to follow, to a certain extent and as long as may seem to me necessary, their indications and even their directions, it is because their authority is imposed upon me by no one, neither by men nor by God. Otherwise I would repel them with horror, and bid the devil take their counsels, their directions, and their services, certain that they would make me pay, by the loss of my liberty and self-respect, for such scraps of truth, wrapped in a multitude of lies, as they might give me.

I bow before the authority of special men because it is imposed upon me by my own reason. I am conscious of my inability to grasp, in all its details and positive developments, any very large portion of human knowledge. The greatest intelligence would not be equal to a comprehension of the whole. Thence results, for science as well as for industry, the necessity of the division and association of labor. I receive and I give—such is human life. Each directs and is directed in his turn. Therefore there is no fixed and constant authority, but a continual exchange of mutual, temporary, and, above all, voluntary authority and subordination.

This same reason forbids me, then, to recognize a fixed, constant, and universal authority, because there is no universal man, no man capable of grasping in that wealth of detail, without which the application of science to life is impossible, all the sciences, all the branches of social life. And if such universality could ever be realized in a single man, and if he wished to take advantage thereof to impose his authority upon us, it would be necessary to drive this man out of society, because his authority would inevitably reduce all the others to slavery and imbecility. I do not think that society ought to maltreat men of genius as it has done hitherto; but neither do I think it should indulge them too far, still less accord them any privileges or exclusive rights whatsoever; and that for three reasons: first, because it would often mistake a charlatan for a man of genius; second, because, through such a system of privileges, it might transform into a charlatan even a real man of genius, demoralize him, and degrade him; and, finally, because it would establish a master over itself.

To sum up. We recognize, then, the absolute authority of science, because the sole object of science is the mental reproduction, as well-considered and systematic as possible, of the natural laws inherent in the material, intellectual, and moral life of both the physical and the social worlds, these two worlds constituting, in fact, but one and the same natural world. Outside of this only legitimate authority, legitimate because rational and in harmony with human liberty, we declare all other authorities false, arbitrary and fatal.

We recognize the absolute authority of science, but we reject the infallibility and universality of the *savant*. In our church—if I may be permitted to use for a moment an expression which I so detest: Church and State are my two *bêtes noires*—in our church, as in the Protestant church, we have a chief, an invisible Christ, science; and, like the Protestants, more logical even than the Protestants, we will suffer neither pope, nor council, nor conclaves of infallible cardinals, nor bishops, nor even priests. Our Christ differs from the Protestant and Christian Christ in this—that the latter is a personal being, ours impersonal; the Christian Christ, already completed in an eternal past, presents himself as a perfect being, while the completion and perfection of our Christ, science, are ever in the future: which is equivalent to saying that they will never be realized. Therefore, in recognizing *absolute science* as the only absolute authority, we in no way compromise our liberty.

I mean by the words "absolute science," the truly universal science which would reproduce ideally, to its fullest extent and in all its infinite detail, the universe, the system or co-ordination of all the natural laws manifested by the incessant development of the world. It is evident that such a science, the sublime object of all the efforts of the human mind, will never be fully and absolutely realized. Our Christ, then, will remain eternally unfinished, which must considerably take down the pride of his licensed representa.tives among us. Against that God the Son in whose name they assume to impose upon us their insolent and pedantic authority, we appeal to God the Father, who is the real world, real life, of which he (the Son) is only a too imperfect expression, whilst we real beings, living, working, struggling, loving, aspiring, enjoying, and suffering, are its immediate representatives.

But, while rejecting the absolute, universal, and infallible authority of men of science, we willingly bow before the respectable, although relative, quite temporary, and very restricted authority of the representatives of special sciences, asking nothing better than to consult them by turns, and very grateful for such precious information as they may extend to us, on condition of their willingness to receive from us on occasions when, and concerning matters about which, we are more learned than they. In general, we ask nothing better than to see men endowed with great knowledge, great experience, great minds, and, above all, great hearts, exercise over us a natural and legitimate influence, freely accepted, and never imposed in the name of any official authority whatsoever, celestial or terrestrial. We accept all natural authorities and all influences of fact, but none of right; for every authority or every influence of right, officially imposed as such, becoming directly an oppression and a falsehood, would inevitably impose upon us, as I believe I have sufficiently shown, slavery and absurdity.

In a word, we reject all legislation, all authority, and all privileged, licensed, official, and legal influence, even though arising from universal suffrage, convinced that it can turn only to the advantage of a dominant minority of exploiters against the interests of the immense majority in subjection to them.

This is the sense in which we are really Anarchists.

The modern idealists understand authority in quite a different way. Although free from the traditional superstitions of all the existing positive religions, they nevertheless attach to this idea of authority a divine, an absolute mean-

ing. This authority is not that of a truth miraculously revealed, nor that of a truth rigorously and scientifically demonstrated. They base it to a slight extent upon quasi-philo-
sophical reasoning, and to a large extent on vaguely religious
faith, to a large extent also on sentiment, ideally, abstractly
poetical. Their religion is, as it were, a last attempt to
divinize all that constitutes humanity in men.

This is just the opposite of the work that we are doing.
In behalf of human liberty, dignity, and prosperity, we believe it our duty to recover from heaven the goods which it
has stolen and return them to earth. They, on the contrary,
endeavoring to commit a final religiously heroic larceny,
would restore to heaven, that divine robber, finally un-
masked, the grandest, finest, and noblest of humanity's pos-
sessions. It is now the freethinkers' turn to pillage heaven
by their audacious impiety and scientific analysis.

The idealists undoubtedly believe that human ideas and
deeds, in order to exercise greater authority among men,
must be invested with a divine sanction. How is this sanction manifested? Not by a miracle, as in the positive religions, but by the very grandeur or sanctity of the ideas
and deeds: whatever is grand, whatever is beautiful, whatever is noble, whatever is just, is considered divine. In this
new religious cult every man inspired by these ideas, by
these deeds, becomes a priest, directly consecrated by God
himself. And the proof? He needs none beyond the very
grandeur of the ideas which he expresses and the deeds
which he performs. These are so holy that they can have
been inspired only by God.

Such, in few words, is their whole philosophy: a philosophy of sentiments, not of real thoughts, a sort of metaphysical pietism. This seems harmless, but it is not so at
all, and the very precise, very narrow, and very barren doctrine hidden under the intangible vagueness of these poetic
forms leads to the same disastrous results that all the positive religions lead to—namely, the most complete negation
of human liberty and dignity.

To proclaim as divine all that is grand, just, noble, and beautiful in humanity is to tacitly admit that humanity of itself would have been unable to produce it—that is, that, abandoned to itself, its own nature is miserable, iniquitous, base, and ugly. Thus we come back to the essence of all religion—in other words, to the disparagement of humanity for the greater glory of divinity. And from the moment that the natural inferiority of man and his fundamental incapacity to rise by his own effort, unaided by any divine inspiration, to the comprehension of just and true ideas, are admitted, it becomes necessary to admit also all the theological, political, and social consequences of the positive religions. From the moment that God, the perfect and supreme being, is posited face to face with humanity, divine mediators, the elect, the inspired of God spring from the earth to enlighten, direct, and govern in his name the human race.

May we not suppose that all men are equally inspired by God? Then, surely, there is no further use for mediators. But this supposition is impossible, because it is too clearly contradicted by the facts. It would compel us to attribute to divine inspiration all the absurdities and errors which appear, and all the horrors, follies, base deeds, and cowardly actions which are committed, in the world. But perhaps, then, only a few men are divinely inspired, the great men of history, the *virtuous geniuses,* as the illustrious Italian citizen and prophet, Giuseppe Mazzini, called them. Immediately inspired by God himself and supported upon universal consent expressed by popular suffrage—*Dio e Popolo*—such as these should be called to the government of human societies.*

But here we are again fallen back under the yoke of

---

*In London I once heard M. Louis Blanc express almost the same idea. "The best form of government," said he to me, "would be that which would invariably call *men of virtuous genius* to the control of affairs."

Church and State. It is true that in this new organization, indebted for its existence, like all the old political organizations, to the *grace of God,* but supported this time—at least so far as form is concerned, as a necessary concession to the spirit of modern times, and just as in the preambles of the imperial decrees of Napoleon III.—on the (pretended) *will of the people,* the Church will no longer call itself Church; it will call itself School. What matters it? On the benches of this School will be seated not children only; there will be found the eternal minor, the pupil confessedly forever incompetent to pass his examinations, rise to the knowledge of his teachers, and dispense with their discipline —the people.* The State will no longer call itself Mon-

---

*One day I asked Mazzini what measures would be taken for the emancipation of the people, once his triumphant unitary republic had been definitely established. "The first measure," he answered, "will be the foundation of schools for the people." "And what will the people be taught in these schools?" "The duties of man—sacrifice and devotion." But where will you find a sufficient number of professors to teach these things, which no one has the right or power to teach, unless he preaches by example? Is not the number of men who find supreme enjoyment in sacrifice and devotion exceedingly limited? Those who sacrifice themselves in the service of a great idea obey a lofty passion, and, *satisfying this personal passion,* outside of which life itself loses all value in their eyes, they generally think of something else than building their action into doctrine, while those who teach doctrine usually forget to translate it into action, for the simple reason that doctrine kills the life, the living spontaneity, of action. Men like Mazzini, in whom doctrine and action form an admirable unity, are very rare exceptions. In Christianity also there have been great men, holy men, who have really practised, or who, at least, have passionately tried to practice all that they preached, and whose hearts, overflowing with love, were full of contempt for the pleasures and goods of this world. But the immense majority of Catholic and Protestant priests who, by trade, have preached and still preach the doctrines of chastity, abstinence, and renunciation belie their teachings by their example. It is not without reason, but because of several centuries' experience, that among the people of all countries these phrases have become by-words: *As licentious as a priest; as gluttonous as a priest; as ambitious as a priest; as greedy, selfish, and*

archy; it will call itself Republic: but it will be none the less the State—that is, a tutelage officially and regularly established by a minority of competent men, *men of virtuous genius or talent,* who will watch and guide the conduct of this great, incorrigible, and terrible child, the people. The professors of the School and the functionaries of the State will call themselves republicans; but they will be none the less tutors, shepherds, and the people will remain what they have been hitherto from all eternity, a flock. Beware of shearers, for where there is a flock there necessarily must be shepherds also to shear and devour it.

The people, in this system, will be the perpetual scholar and pupil. In spite of its sovereignty, wholly fictitious, it

---

grasping as a priest. It is, then, established that the professors of the Christian virtues, consecrated by the Church, the priests, *in the immense majority of cases,* have practised quite the contrary of what they have preached. This very majority, the universality of this fact, show that the fault is not to be attributed to them as individuals, but to the social position, impossible and contradictory in itself, in which these individuals are placed. The position of the Christian priest involves a double contradiction. In the first place, that between the doctrine of abstinence and renunciation and the positive tendencies and needs of human nature—tendencies and needs which, in some individual cases, always very rare, may indeed be continually held back, suppressed, and even entirely annihilated by the constant influence of some potent intellectual and moral passion; which at certain moments of collective exaltation, may be forgotten and neglected for some time by a large mass of men at once; but which are so fundamentally inherent in our nature that sooner or later they always resume their rights: so that, when they are not satisfied in a regular and normal way, they are always replaced at last by unwholesome and monstrous satisfaction. This is a natural and consequently fatal and irresistible law, under the disastrous action of which inevitably fall all Christian priests and especially those of the Roman Catholic Church. It cannot apply to the professors, that is to the priests of the modern Church, unless they are also obliged to preach Christian abstinence and renunciation.

But there is another contradiction common to the priests of both sects. This contradiction grows out of the very title and position of master. A master who commands, oppresses, and exploits is a wholly logical and quite natural personage. But a master who will continue to serve as the instrument of thoughts, wills, and consequently interests not its own. Between this situation and what we call liberty, the only real liberty, there is an abyss. It will be the old oppression and old slavery under new forms; and where there is slavery there is misery, brutishness, real social *materialism,* among the privileged classes as well as among the masses.

In deifying human things the idealists always end in the triumph of a brutal materialism. And this for a very simple reason: the divine evaporates and rises to its own country, heaven, while the brutal alone remains actually on earth.

Yes, the necessary consequence of theoretical idealism is

---

sacrifices himself to those who are subordinated to him by his divine or human privilege is a contradictory and quite impossible being. This is the very constitution of hypocrisy, so well personified by the Pope, who, while calling himself *the lowest servant of the servants of God*—in token whereof, following the example of Christ, he even washes once a year the feet of twelve Roman beggars—proclaims himself at the same time vicar of God, absolute and infallible master of the world. Do I need to recall that the priests of all churches, far from sacrificing themselves to the flocks confided to their care, have always sacrificed them, exploited them, and kept them in the condition of a flock, partly to satisfy their own personal passions and partly to serve the omnipotence of the Church? Like conditions, like causes, always produce like effects. It will, then, be the same with the professors of the modern School divinely inspired and licensed by the State. They will necessarily become, some without knowing it, others with full knowledge of the cause, teachers of the doctrine of popular sacrifice to the power of the State and to the profit of the privileged classes.

Must we, then, eliminate from society all instruction and abolish all schools? Far from it! Instruction must be spread among the masses without stint, transforming all the churches, all those temples dedicated to the glory of God and to the slavery of men, into so many schools of human emancipation. But, in the first place, let us understand each other; schools, properly speaking, in a normal society founded on equality and on respect for human liberty, will exist only for children and not for adults; and, in order that they may become schools of emancipation and not of enslavement, it will be necessary to eliminate, first of all, this fiction of God, the eternal and absolute enslaver. The whole education of children

practically the most brutal materialism; not, undoubtedly, among those who sincerely preach it—the usual result as far as they are concerned being that they are constrained to see all their efforts struck with sterility—but among those who try to realize their precepts in life, and in all society so far as it allows itself to be dominated by idealistic doctrines.

To demonstrate this general fact, which may appear strange at first, but which explains itself naturally enough upon further reflection, historical proofs are not lacking.

Compare the last two civilizations of the ancient world— the Greek and the Roman. Which is the most materialistic,

---

and their instruction must be founded on the scientific development of reason, not on that of faith; on the development of personal dignity and independence, not on that of piety and obedience; on the worship of truth and justice at any cost, and above all on respect for humanity, which must replace always and everywhere the worship of divinity. The principle of authority, in the education of children, constitutes the natural point of departure; it is legitimate, necessary, when applied to children of a tender age, whose intelligence has not yet openly developed itself. But as the development of everything, and consequently of education, implies the gradual negation of the point of departure, this principle must diminish as fast as education and instruction advance, giving place to increasing liberty. All rational education is at bottom nothing but this progressive immolation of authority for the benefit of liberty, the final object of education necessarily being the formation of free men full of respect and love for the liberty of others. Therefore the first day of the pupils' life, if the school takes infants scarcely able as yet to stammer a few words, should be that of the greatest authority and an almost entire absence of liberty; but its last day should be that of the greatest liberty and the absolute abolition of every vestige of the animal or divine principle of authority.

The principle of authority, applied to men who have surpassed or attained their majority, becomes a monstrosity, a flagrant denial of humanity, a source of slavery and intellectual and moral depravity. Unfortunately, paternal governments have left the masses to wallow in an ignorance so profound that it will be necessary to establish schools not only for the people's children, but for the people themselves. From these schools will be absolutely

the most natural, in its point of departure, and the most humanly ideal in its results? Undoubtedly the Greek civilization. Which on the contrary, is the most abstractly ideal in its point of departure—sacrificing the material liberty of the man to the ideal liberty of the citizen, represented by the abstraction of judicial law, and the natural development of human society to the abstraction of the State—and which became nevertheless the most brutal in its consequences? The Roman civilization, certainly. It is true that the Greek civilization, like all the ancient civilizations, including that of Rome, was exclusively national and based on slavery. But, in spite of these two immense defects, the former none

---

eliminated the smallest applications or manifestations of the principle of authority. They will be schools no longer; they will be popular academies, in which neither pupils nor masters will be known, where the people will come freely to get, if they need it, free instruction, and in which, rich in their own experience, they will teach in their turn many things to the professors who shall bring them knowledge which they lack. This, then, will be a mutual instruction, an act of intellectual fraternity between the educated youth and the people.

The real school for the people and for all grown men is life. The only grand and omnipotent authority, at once natural and rational, the only one which we may respect, will be that of the collective and public spirit of a society founded on equality and solidarity and the mutual human respect of all its members. Yes, this is an authority which is not at all divine, wholly human, but before which we shall bow willingly, certain that, far from enslaving them, it will emancipate men. It will be a thousand times more powerful, be sure of it, than all your divine, theological, metaphysical, political, and judicial authorities, established by the Church and by the State; more powerful than your criminal codes, your jailers, and your executioners.

The power of collective sentiment or public spirit is even now a very serious matter. The men most ready to commit crimes rarely dare to defy it, to openly affront it. They will seek to deceive it, but will take care not to be rude with it unless they feel the support of a minority larger or smaller. No man, however powerful he believes himself, will ever have the strength to bear the unanimous contempt of society; no one can live without feeling himself sustained by the approval and esteem of at least some

the less conceived and realized the idea of humanity; it ennobled and really idealized the life of men; it transformed human herds into free associations of free men; it created through liberty the sciences, the arts, a poetry, an immortal philosophy, and the primary concepts of human respect. With political and social liberty, it created free thought. At the close of the Middle Ages, during the period of the Renaissance, the fact that some Greek emigrants brought a few of those immortal books into Italy sufficed to resuscitate life, liberty, thought, humanity, buried in the dark dungeon of Catholicism. Human emancipation, that is the name of the Greek civilization. And the name of the Roman civilization? Conquest, with all its brutal consequences.

---

portion of society. A man must be urged on by an immense and very sincere conviction in order to find courage to speak and act against the opinion of all, and never will a selfish, depraved, and cowardly man have such courage.

Nothing proves more clearly than this fact the natural and inevitable solidarity—this law of sociability—which binds all men together, as each of us can verify daily, both on himself and on all the men whom he knows. But, if this social power exists, why has it not sufficed hitherto to moralize, to humanize men? Simply because hitherto this power has not been humanized itself; it has not been humanized because the social life of which it is ever the faithful expression is based, as we know, on the worship of divinity, not on respect for humanity; on authority, not on liberty; on privilege, not on equality; on the exploitation, not on the brotherhood of men; on iniquity and falsehood, not on justice and truth. Consequently its real action, always in contradiction of the humanitarian theories which it professes, has constantly exercised a disastrous and depraving influence. It does not repress vices and crimes; it creates them. Its authority is consequently a divine, anti-human authority; its influence is mischievous and baleful. Do you wish to render its authority and influence beneficent and human? Achieve the social revolution. Make all needs really solidary, and cause the material and social interests of each to conform to the human duties of each. And to this end there is but one means: Destroy all the institutions of Inequality; establish the economic and social equality of all, and on this basis will arise the liberty, the morality, the solidary humanity of all.

I shall return to this, the most important question of Socialism.

And its last word? The omnipotence of the Cæsars. Which means the degradation and enslavement of nations and of men.

To-day even, what is it that kills, what is it that crushes brutally, materially, in all European countries, liberty and humanity? It is the triumph of the Cæsarian or Roman principle.

Compare now two modern civilizations—the Italian and the German. The first undoubtedly represents, in its general character, materialism; the second, on the contrary, represents idealism in its most abstract, most pure, and most transcendental form. Let us see what are the practical fruits of the one and the other.

Italy has already rendered immense services to the cause of human emancipation. She was the first to resuscitate and widely apply the principle of liberty in Europe, and to restore to humanity its titles to nobility: industry, commerce, poetry, the arts, the positive sciences, and free thought. Crushed since by three centuries of imperial and papal despotism, and dragged in the mud by her governing bourgeoisie, she reappears to-day, it is true, in a very degraded condition in comparison with what she once was. And yet how much she differs from Germany! In Italy, in spite of this decline—temporary let us hope—one may live and breathe humanly, surrounded by a people which seems to be born for liberty. Italy, even bourgeois Italy, can point with pride to men like Mazzini and Garibaldi. In Germany one breathes the atmosphere of an immense political and social slavery, philosophically explained and accepted by a great people with deliberate resignation and free will. Her heroes—I speak always of present Germany, not of the Germany of the future; of aristocratic, bureaucratic, political and bourgeoise Germany, not of the Germany of the *prolétaires*—her heroes are quite the opposite of Mazzini and Garibaldi: they are William I., that ferocious and ingenuous representative of the Protestant God, Messrs. Bismarck and Moltke, Generals Manteuffel and

Werder. In all her international relations Germany, from the beginning of her existence, has been slowly, systematically invading, conquering, ever ready to extend. her own voluntary enslavement into the territory of her neighbors; and, since her definitive establishment as a unitary power, she has become a menace, a danger to the liberty of entire Europe. To-day Germany is servility brutal and triumphant.

To show how theoretical idealism incessantly and inevitably changes into practical materialism, one needs only to cite the example of all the Christian Churches, and, naturally, first of all, that of the Apostolic and Roman Church. What is there more sublime, in the ideal sense, more disinterested, more separate from all the interests of this earth, than the doctrine of Christ preached by that Church? And what is there more brutally materialistic than the constant practice of that same Church since the eighth century, from which dates her definitive establishment as a power? What has been and still is the principal object of all her contests with the sovereigns of Europe? Her temporal goods, her revenues first, and then her temporal power, her political privileges. We must do her the justice to acknowledge that she was the first to discover, in modern history, this incontestable but scarcely Christian truth that wealth and power, the economic exploitation and the political oppression of the masses, are the two inseparable terms of the reign of divine ideality on earth: wealth consolidating and augmenting power, power ever discovering and creating new sources of wealth, and both assuring, better than the martyrdom and faith of the apostles, better than divine grace, the success of the Christian propagandism. This is a historical truth, and the Protestant Churches do not fail to recognize it either. I speak, of course, of the independent churches of England, America, and Switzerland, not of the subjected churches of Germany. The latter have no initiative of their own; they do what their masters, their temporal sovereigns, who are at the same time their spiritual chieftains, order them to do, It is well known that the Protestant propagandism, especially in England and America, is very intimately connected with the propagandism of the material, commercial interests of those two great nations; and it is known also that the objects of the latter propagandism is not at all the enrichment and material prosperity of the countries into which it penetrates in company with the Word of God, but rather the exploitation of those countries with a view to the enrichment and material prosperity of certain classes, which in their own country are very covetous and very pious at the same time.

In a word, it is not at all difficult to prove, history in hand, that the Church, that all the Churches, Christian and non-Christian, by the side of their spiritualistic propagandism, and probably to accelerate and consolidate the success thereof, have never neglected to organize themselves into great corporations for the economic exploitation of the masses under the protection and with the direct and special blessing of some divinity or other; that all the States, which originally, as we know, with all their political and judicial institutions and their dominant and privileged classes, have been only temporal branches of these various Churches, have likewise had principally in view this same exploitation for the benefit of lay minorities indirectly sanctioned by the Church; finally and in general, that the action of the good God and of all the divine idealities on earth has ended at last, always and everywhere, in founding the prosperous materialism of the few over the fanatical and constantly famishing idealism of the masses.

We have a new proof of this in what we see to-day. With the exception of the great hearts and great minds whom I have before referred to as misled, who are to-day the most obstinate defenders of idealism? In the first place, all the sovereign courts. In France, until lately, Napoleon III. and his wife, Madame Eugénie; all their former ministers, courtiers, and ex-marshals, from Rouher and Bazaine to Fleury and Piétri; the men and women of this imperial world, who have so completely idealized and saved France;

their journalists and their *savants*—the Cassagnacs, the Girardins, the Duvernois, the Veuillots, the Leverriers, the Dumas; the black phalanx of Jesuits and Jesuitesses in every garb; the whole upper and middle bourgeoisie of France; the doctrinaire liberals, and the liberals without doctrine—the Guizots, the Thiers, the Jules Favres, the Pelletans, and the Jules Simons, all obstinate defenders of the bourgeoise exploitation. In Prussia, in Germany, William I., the present royal demonstrator of the good God on earth; all his generals, all his officers, Pomeranian and other; all his army, which, strong in its religious faith, has just conquered France in that ideal way we know so well. In Russia, the Czar and his court; the Mouravieffs and the Bergs, all the butchers and pious proselyters of Poland. Everywhere, in short, religious or philosophical idealism, the one being but the more or less free translation of the other, serves to-day as the flag of material, bloody, and brutal force, of shameless material exploitation; while, on the contrary, the flag of theoretical materialism, the red flag of economic equality and social justice, is raised by the practical idealism of the oppressed and famishing masses, tending to realize the greatest liberty and the human right of each in the fraternity of all men on the earth.

Who are the real idealists—the idealists not of abstraction, but of life, not of heaven, but of earth—and who are the materialists?

It is evident that the essential condition of theoretical or divine idealism is the sacrifice of logic, of human reason, the renunciation of science. We see, further, that in defending the doctrines of idealism one finds himself enlisted perforce in the ranks of the oppressors and exploiters of the masses. These are two great reasons which, it would seem, should be sufficient to drive every great mind, every great heart, from idealism. How does it happen that our illustrious contemporary idealists, who certainly lack neither mind, nor heart, nor good will, and who have devoted their entire existence to the service of humanity—how does it happen that they persist in remaining among the representatives of a doctrine henceforth condemned and dishonored?

They must be influenced by a very powerful motive. It cannot be logic or science, since logic and science have pronounced their verdict against the idealistic doctrine. No more can it be personal interests, since these men are infinitely above everything of that sort. It must, then, be a powerful moral motive. Which? There can be but one. These illustrious men think, no doubt, that idealistic theories or beliefs are essentially necessary to the moral dignity and grandeur of man, and that materialistic theories, on the contrary, reduce him to the level of the beasts.

And if the truth were just the opposite!

Every development, I have said, implies the negation of its point of departure. The basis or point of departure, according to the materialistic school, being material, the negation must be necessarily ideal. Starting from the totality of the real world, or from what is abstractly called matter, it logically arrives at the real idealization—that is, at the humanization, at the full and complete emancipation—of society. *Per contra* and for the same reason, the basis and point of departure of the idealistic school being ideal, it arrives necessarily at the materialization of society, at the organization of a brutal despotism and an iniquitous and ignoble exploitation, under the form of Church and State. The historical development of man according to the materialistic school, is a progressive ascension; in the idealistic system it can be nothing but a continuous fall.

Whatever human question we may desire to consider, we always find this same essential contradiction between the two schools. Thus, as I have already observed, materialism starts from animality to establish humanity; idealism starts from divinity to establish slavery and condemn the masses to an endless animality. Materialism denies free will and ends in the establishment of liberty; idealism, in the name of human dignity, proclaims free will, and on the ruins of every liberty founds authority. Materialism rejects the principle of authority, because it rightly considers it as the corollary of animality, and because, on the contrary, the triumph of humanity, the object and chief significance of history, can be realized only through liberty. In a word, you will always find the idealists in the very act of practical materialism, while you will see the materialists pursuing and realizing the most grandly ideal aspirations and thoughts.

History, in the system of the idealists, as I have said, can be nothing but a continuous fall. They begin by a terrible fall, from which they never recover—by the *salto mortale* from the sublime regions of pure and absolute idea into matter. And into what kind of matter! Not into the matter which is eternally active and mobile, full of properties and forces, of life and intelligence, as we see it in the real world; but into abstract matter, impoverished and reduced to absolute misery by the regular looting of these Prussians of thought, the theologians and metaphysicians, who have stripped it of everything to give everything to their emperor, to their God; into the matter which, deprived of all action and movement of its own, represents, in opposition to the divine idea, nothing but absolute stupidity, impenetrability, inertia and immobility.

The fall is so terrible that divinity, the divine person or idea, is flattened out, loses consciousness of itself, and never more recovers it. And in this desperate situation it is still forced to work miracles! For from the moment that matter becomes inert, every movement that takes place in the world, even the most material, is a miracle, can result only from a providential intervention, from the action of God upon matter. And there this poor Divinity, degraded and half annihilated by its fall, lies some thousands of centuries in this swoon, then awakens slowly, in vain endeavoring to grasp some vague memory of itself, and every move that it makes in this direction upon matter becomes a creation, a new formation, a new miracle. In this way it passes through all degrees of materiality and bestiality—first, gas, simple or compound chemical substance, mineral, it then spreads over the earth as vegetable and animal organization till it concentrates itself in man. Here it would seem as if it must become itself again, for it lights in every human being an angelic spark, a particle of its own divine being, the immortal soul.

How did it manage to lodge a thing absolutely immaterial in a thing absolutely material; how can the body contain, enclose, limit, paralyze pure spirit? This, again, is one of those questions which faith alone, that passionate and stupid affirmation of the absurd, can solve. It is the greatest of miracles. Here, however, we have only to establish the effects, the practical consequences of this miracle.

After thousands of centuries of vain efforts to come back to itself, Divinity, lost and scattered in the matter which it animates and sets in motion, finds a point of support, a sort of focus for self-concentration. This focus is man, his immortal soul singularly imprisoned in a mortal body. But each man considered individually is infinitely too limited, too small, to enclose the divine immensity; it can contain only a very small particle, immortal like the whole, but infinitely smaller than the whole. It follows that the divine being, the absolutely immaterial being, mind, is divisible like matter. Another mystery whose solution must be left to faith.

If God entire could find lodgment in each man, then each man would be God. We should have an immense quantity of Gods, each limited by all the others and yet none the less infinite—a contradiction which would imply a mutual destruction of men, an impossibility of the existence of more than one. As for the particles, that is another matter; nothing more rational, indeed, than that one particle should be limited by another and be smaller than the whole. Only, here another contradiction confronts us. To be limited, to be greater and smaller are attributes of matter, not of mind. According to the materialists, it is true, mind is only the working of the wholly material organism of man, and the greatness or smallness of mind depends absolutely on the greater or less material perfection of the human organism.

But these same attributes of relative limitation and grandeur cannot be attributed to mind as the idealists conceive it, absolutely immaterial mind, mind existing independent of matter. There can be neither greater nor smaller nor any limit among minds, for there is only one mind—God. To add that the infinitely small and limited particles which constitute human souls are at the same time immortal is to carry the contradiction to a climax. But this is a question of faith. Let us pass on.

Here then we have Divinity torn up and lodged, in infinitely small particles, in an immense number of beings of all sexes, ages, races, and colors. This is an excessively inconvenient and unhappy situation, for the divine particles are so little acquainted with each other at the outset of their human existence that they begin by devouring each other. Moreover, in the midst of this state of barbarism and wholly animal brutality, these divine particles, human souls, retain as it were a vague remembrance of their primitive divinity, and are irresistibly drawn towards their whole; they seek each other, they seek their whole. It is Divinity itself, scattered and lost in the natural world, which looks for itself in men, and it is so demolished by this multitude of human prisons in which it finds itself strewn, that, in looking for itself, it commits folly after folly.

Beginning with fetichism, it searches for and adores itself, now in a stone, now in a piece of wood, now in a rag. It is quite likely that it would never have succeeded in getting out of the rag, if *the other* divinity which was not allowed to fall into matter and which is kept in a state of pure spirit in the sublime heights of the absolute ideal, or in the celestial regions, had not had pity on it.

Here is a new mystery—that of Divinity dividing itself into two halves, both equally infinite, of which one—God the Father—stays in the purely immaterial regions, and the other—God the Son—falls into matter. We shall see directly, between these two Divinities separated from each other, continuous relations established, from above to below and from below to above; and these relations, considered as a single eternal and constant act, will constitute the Holy Ghost. Such, in its veritable theological and metaphysical meaning, is the great, the terrible mystery of the Christian Trinity.

But let us lose no time in abandoning these heights to see what is going on upon earth.

God the Father, seeing from the height of his eternal splendor that the poor God the Son, flattened out and astounded by his fall, is so plunged and lost in matter that even having reached human state he has not yet recovered himself, decides to come to his aid. From this immense number of particles at once immortal, divine, and infinitely small, in which God the Son has disseminated himself so thoroughly that he does not know himself, God the Father chooses those most pleasing to him, picks his inspired persons, his prophets, his "men of virtuous genius," the great benefactors and legislators of humanity: Zoroaster, Buddha, Moses, Confucius, Lycurgus, Solon, Socrates, the divine Plato, and above all Jesus Christ, the complete realization of God the Son, at last collected and concentrated in a single human person; all the apostles, Saint Peter, Saint Paul, and Saint John before all, Constantine the Great, Mahomet, then Charlemagne, Gregory VII., Dante, and, according to some, Luther also, Voltaire and Rousseau, Robespierre and Danton, and many other great and holy historical personages, all of whose names it is impossible to recapitulate, but among whom I, as a Russian, beg that Saint Nicholas may not be forgotten.

Then we have reached at last the manifestation of God upon earth. But immediately God appears, man is reduced to nothing. It will be said that he is not reduced to nothing, since he is himself a particle of God. Pardon me! I admit that a particle of a definite, limited whole, however small it be, is a quantity, a positive greatness. But a particle of the infinitely great, compared with it, is necessarily infinitely small. Multiply milliards of milliards by milliards of milliards—their product compared to the infinitely great, will be infinitely small, and the infinitely small is equal to zero. God is everything; therefore man and all the real world with him, the universe, are nothing. You will not escape this conclusion.

God appears, man is reduced to nothing; and the greater Divinity becomes, the more miserable becomes humanity. That is the history of all religions; that is the effect of all the divine inspirations and legislations. In history the name of God is the terrible club with which all divinely inspired men, the great "virtuous geniuses," have beaten down the liberty, dignity, reason, and prosperity of man.

We had first the fall of God. Now we have a fall which interests us more—that of man, caused solely by the apparition of God manifested on earth.

See in how profound an error our dear and illustrious idealists find themselves. In talking to us of God they purpose, they desire, to elevate us, emancipate us, ennoble us, and, on the contrary, they crush and degrade us. With the name of God they imagine that they can establish fraternity among men, and, on the contrary, they create pride, contempt; they sow discord, hatred, war; they establish slavery. For with God come the different degrees of divine inspiration; humanity is divided into men highly inspired, less inspired, uninspired. All are equally insignificant before God, it is true; but, compared with each other, some are greater than others; not only in fact—which would be of no consequence, because inequality in fact is lost in the collectivity when it cannot cling to some legal fiction or institution— but by the divine right of inspiration, which immediately establishes a fixed, constant, petrifying inequality. The highly inspired *must* be listened to and obeyed by the less inspired, and the less inspired by the uninspired. Thus we have the principle of authority well established, and with it the two fundamental institutions of slavery: Church and State.

Of all despotisms that of the *doctrinaires* or inspired religionists is the worst. They are so jealous of the glory of their God and of the triumph of their idea that they have no heart left for the liberty or the dignity or even the sufferings of living men, of real men. Divine zeal, preoccupation with the idea, finally dry up the tenderest souls, the most compassionate hearts, the sources of human love. Considering all that is, all that happens in the world from the point of view of eternity or of the abstract idea, they treat passing matters with disdain; but the whole life of real men, of men of flesh and bone, is composed only of passing matters; they themselves are only passing beings, who, once passed, are replaced by others likewise passing, but never to return in person. Alone permanent or relatively eternal in men is humanity, which steadily developing, grows richer in passing from one generation to another. I say *relatively* eternal, because, our planet once destroyed—it cannot fail to perish sooner or later, since everything which has begun must necessarily end—our planet once decomposed, to serve undoubtedly as an element of some new formation in the system of the universe, which alone is really eternal, who knows what will become of our whole human development? Nevertheless, the moment of this dissolution being an enormous distance in the future, we may properly consider humanity, relatively to the short duration of human life, as eternal. But this very fact of progressive humanity is real and living only through its manifestations at definite times, in definite places, in really living men, and not through its general idea.

The general idea is always an abstraction and, for that very reason, in some sort a negation of real life. I have stated in the Appendix that human thought and, in consequence of this, science can grasp and name only the general significance of real facts, their relations, their laws—in short, that which is permanent in their continual transformations —but never their material, individual side, palpitating, so to speak, with reality and life, and therefore fugitive and intangible. Science comprehends the thought of the reality, not reality itself; the thought of life, not life. That is its

limit, its only really insuperable limit, because it is founded
on the very nature of thought, which is the only organ of
science.

Upon this nature are based the indisputable rights and
grand mission of science, but also its vital impotence and
even its mischievous action whenever, through its official
licensed representatives, it arrogantly claims the right to
govern life. The mission of science is, by observation of the
general relations of passing and real facts, to establish the
general laws inherent in the development of the phenomena
of the physical and social world; it fixes, so to speak, the
unchangeable landmarks of humanity's progressive march
by indicating the general conditions which it is necessary to
rigorously observe and always fatal to ignore or forget. In
a word, science is the compass of life; but it is not life.
Science is unchangeable, impersonal, general, abstract, in-
sensible, like the laws of which it is but the ideal reproduction, reflected or mental—that is cerebral (using this word
to remind us that science itself is but a material product of
a material organ, the *brain*). Life is wholly fugitive and
temporary, but also wholly palpitating with reality and individuality, sensibility, sufferings, joys, aspirations, needs,
and passions. It alone spontaneously creates real things and
beings. Science creates nothing; it establishes and recog-
nizes only the creations of life. And every time that scientific men, emerging from their abstract world, mingle with
living creation in the real world, all that they propose or
create is poor, ridiculously abstract, bloodless and lifeless,
still-born, like the *homunculus* created by Wagner, the pedantic disciple of the immortal Doctor Faust. It follows that
the only mission of science is to enlighten life, not to govern it.

The government of science and of men of science, even
be they positivists, disciples of Auguste Comte, or, again,
disciples of the *doctrinaire* school of German Communism,
cannot fail to be impotent, ridiculous, inhuman, cruel, oppressive, exploiting, maleficent. We may say of men of

science, *as such,* what I have said of theologians and meta-physicians: they have neither sense nor heart for individual and living beings. We cannot even blame them for this, for it is the natural consequence of their profession. In so far as they are men of science, they have to deal with and can take interest in nothing except generalities; that do the laws*.   .   .   .   .
.   .   .   .

.   .   .   .   they are not exclusively men of science, but are also more or less men of life.†

Nevertheless, we must not rely too much on this. Though we may be well nigh certain that a *savant* would not dare to treat a man to-day as he treats a rabbit, it remains always to be feared that the *savants* as a body, if not interfered with, may submit living men to scientific experiments, undoubtedly less cruel but none the less disagreeable to their victims. If they cannot perform experiments upon the bodies of individuals, they will ask nothing better than to perform them on the social body, and that is what must be absolutely prevented.

In their existing organization, monopolizing science and remaining thus outside of social life, the *savants* form a separate caste, in many respects analogous to the priesthood. Scientific abstraction is their God, living and real individuals are their victims, and they are the consecrated and licensed sacrificers.

Science cannot go outside of the sphere of abstractions. In this respect it is infinitely inferior to art, which, in its turn, is peculiarly concerned also with general types and general situations, but which incarnates them by an artifice of

---

*Here three pages of Bakunin's manuscript are missing.

†The lost part of this sentence perhaps said: "If men of science, in their researches and experiments are not treating men actually as they treat animals, the reason is that" they are not exclusively men of science, but are also more or less men of life.

its own in forms which, if they are not living in the sense of real life, none the less excite in our imagination the memory and sentiment of life; art in a certain sense individualizes the types and situations which it conceives; by means of the individualities without flesh and bone, and consequently permanent and immortal, which it has the power to create, it recalls to our minds the living, real individualities which appear and disappear under our eyes. Art, then, is as it were the return of abstraction to life; science, on the contrary, is the perpetual immolation of life, fugitive, temporary, but real, on the altar of eternal abstractions.

Science is as incapable of grasping the individuality of a man as that of a rabbit, being equally indifferent to both. Not that it is ignorant of the principle of individuality: it conceives it perfectly as a principle, but not as a fact. It knows very well that all the animal species, including the human species, have no real existence outside of an indefinite number of individuals, born and dying to make room for new individuals equally fugitive. It knows that in rising from the animal species to the superior species the principle of individuality becomes more pronounced; the individuals appear freer and more complete. It knows that man, the last and most perfect animal of earth, presents the most complete and most remarkable individuality, because of his power to conceive, concrete, personify, as it were, in his social and private existence, the universal law. It knows, finally, when it is not vitiated by theological or metaphysical, political or judcial *doctrinairisme,* or even by a narrow scientific pride, when it is not deaf to the instincts and spontaneous aspirations of life—it knows (and this is its last word) that respect for man is the supreme law of Humanity, and that the great, the real object of history, its only legitimate object, is the humanization and emancipation, the real liberty, the prosperity and happiness of each individual living in society. For, if we would not fall back into the liberticidal fiction of the public welfare represented by the State, a fiction always founded on the systematic sacrifice of the people, we must clearly recognize that collective liberty and prosperity exist only so far as they represent the sum of individual liberties and prosperities.

Science knows all these things, but it does not and cannot go beyond them. Abstraction being its very nature, it can well enough conceive the principle of real and living individuality, but it can have no dealings with real and living individuals; it concerns itself with individuals in general, but not with Peter or James, not with such or such a one, who, so far as it is concerned, do not, cannot, have any existence. Its individuals, I repeat, are only abstractions.

Now, history is made, not by abstract individuals, but by acting, living and passing individuals. Abstractions advance only when borne forward by real men. For these beings made, not in idea only, but in reality of flesh and blood, science has no heart: it considers them at most as *material for intellectual and social development*. What does it care for the particular conditions and chance fate of Peter or James? It would make itself ridiculous, it would abdicate, it would annihilate itself, if it wished to concern itself with them otherwise than as examples in support of its eternal theories. And it would be ridiculous to wish it to do so, for its mission lies not there. It cannot grasp the concrete; it can move only in abstractions. Its mission is to busy itself with the situation and the *general* conditions of the existence and development, either of the human species in general, or of such a race, such a people, such a class or category of individuals; the *general* causes of their prosperity, their decline, and the best *general* methods of securing their progress in all ways. Provided it accomplishes this task broadly and rationally, it will do its whole duty, and it would be really unjust to expect more of it.

But it would be equally ridiculous, it would be disastrous to entrust it with a mission which it is incapable of fulfilling. Since its own nature forces it to ignore the existence of Peter and James, it must never be permitted, nor must anybody be permitted in its name, to govern Peter and James.

For it were capable of treating them almost as it treats rabbits. Or rather, it would continue to ignore them; but its licensed representatives, men not at all abstract, but on the contrary in very active life and having very substantial interests, yielding to the pernicious influence which privilege inevitably exercises upon men, would finally fleece other men in the name of science, just as they have been fleeced hitherto by priests, politicians of all shades, and lawyers, in the name of God, of the State, of judicial Right.

What I preach then is, to a certain extent, the *revolt of life against science,* or rather against the *government of science,* not to destroy science—that would be high treason to humanity—but to remand it to its place so that it can never leave it again. Until now all human history has been only a perpetual and bloody immolation of millions of poor human beings in honor of some pitiless abstraction—God, country, power of State, national honor, historical rights, judicial rights, political liberty, public welfare. Such has been up to-day the natural, spontaneous, and inevitable movement of human societies. We cannot undo it; we must submit to it so far as the past is concerned, as we submit to all natural fatalities. We must believe that that was the only possible way to educate the human race. For we must not deceive ourselves: even in attributing the larger part to the Machiavellian wiles of the governing classes, we have to recognize that no minority would have been powerful enough to impose all these horrible sacrifices upon the masses if there had not been in the masses themselves a dizzy spontaneous movement which pushed them on to continual self-sacrifice, now to one, now to another of these devouring abstractions, the vampires of history, ever nourished upon human blood.

We readily understand that this is very gratifying to the theologians, politicians, and jurists. Priests of these abstractions, they live only by the continual immolation of the people. Nor is it more surprising that metaphysics, too, should give its consent. Its only mission is to justify and rationalize as far as possible the iniquitous and absurd. But that positive science itself should have shown the same tendencies is a fact which we must deplore while we establish it. That it has done so is due to two reasons: in the first place, because, constituted outside of life, it is represented by a privileged body; and in the second place, because thus far it has posited itself as an absolute and final object of all human development. By a judicious criticism, which it can and finally will be forced to pass upon itself, it would understand, on the contrary, that it is only a means for the realization of a much higher object—that of the complete humanization of the *real* situation of all the *real* individuals who are born, who live, and who die, on earth.

The immense advantage of positive science over theology, metaphysics, politics, and judicial right consists in this— that, in place of the false and fatal abstractions set up by these doctrines, it posits true abstractions which express the general nature and logic of things, their general relations, and the general laws of their development. This separates it profoundly from all preceding doctrines, and will assure it for ever a great position in society: it will constitute in a certain sense society's collective consciousness. But there is one aspect in which it resembles all these doctrines: its only possible object being abstractions, it is forced by its very nature to ignore real men, outside of whom the truest abstractions have no existence. To remedy this radical defect positive science will have to proceed by a different method from that followed by the doctrines of the past. The latter have taken advantage of the ignorance of the masses to sacrifice them with delight to their abstractions, which, by the way, are always very lucrative to those who represent them in flesh and bone. Positive science, recognizing its absolute inability to conceive real individuals and interest itself in their lot, must definitely and absolutely renounce all claim to the government of societies; for if it should meddle therein, it would only sacrifice continually the living men whom it ignores to the abstractions which constitute the sole object of its legitimate preoccupations.

The true science of history, for instance, does not yet exist; scarcely do we begin to-day to catch a glimpse of its extremely complicated conditions. But suppose it were definitely developed, what could it give us? It would exhibit a faithful and rational picture of the natural development of the general conditions—material and ideal, economical, political and social, religious, philosophical, æsthetic, and scientific—of the societies which have a history. But this universal picture of human civilization, however detailed it might be, would never show anything beyond general and consequently *abstract* estimates. The milliards of individuals who have furnished the *living and suffering materials* of this history at once triumphant and dismal—triumphant by its general results, dismal by the immense hecatomb of human victims "crushed under its car"—those milliards of obscure individuals without whom none of the great abstract results of history would have been obtained—and who, bear in mind, have never benefited by any of these results—will find no place, not even the slightest, in our annals. They have lived and been sacrificed, crushed for the good of abstract humanity, that is all.

Shall we blame the science of history? That would be unjust and ridiculous. Individuals cannot be grasped by thought, by reflection, or even by human speech, which is capable of expressing abstractions only; they cannot be grasped in the present day any more than in the past. Therefore social science itself, the science of the future, will necessarily continue to ignore them. All that we have a right to demand of it is that it shall point us with faithful and sure hand to the *general causes of individual suffering*—among these causes it will not forget the immolation and subordination (still too frequent, alas!) of living individuals to abstract generalities—at the same time showing us the *general conditions necessary to the real emancipation of the individuals living in society*. That is its mission; those are its limits, beyond which the action of social science can be only impotent and fatal. Beyond those limits being the *doctrinaire* and governmental pretentions of its licensed representatives, its priests. It is time to have done with all popes and priests; we want them no longer, even if they call themselves Social Democrats.

Once more, the sole mission of science is to light the road. Only Life, delivered from all its governmental and *doctrinaire* barriers, and given full liberty of action, can create.

How solve this antinomy?

On the one hand, science is indispensable to the rational organization of society; on the other, being incapable of interesting itself in that which is real and living, it must not interfere with the real or practical organization of society.

This contradiction can be solved only in one way: by the liquidation of science as a moral being existing outside the life of all, and represented by a body of breveted *savants;* it must spread among the masses. Science, being called upon to henceforth represent society's collective consciousness, must really become the property of everybody. Thereby, without losing anything of its universal character, of which it can never divest itself without ceasing to be science, and while continuing to concern itself exclusively with general causes, the conditions and fixed relations of individuals and things, it will become one in fact with the immediate and real life of all individuals. That will be a movement analogous to that which said to the Protestants at the beginning of the Reformation that there was no further need of priests for man, who would henceforth be his own priest, every man, thanks to the invisible intervention of the Lord Jesus Christ alone, having at last succeeded in swallowing his good God. But here the question is not of Jesus Christ, nor good God, nor of political liberty, nor of judicial right—things all theologically or metaphysically revealed, and all alike indigestible. The world of scientific abstractions is not revealed; it is inherent in the real world, of which it is only the general or abstract expression and representation. As long as it forms a separate region, specially represented by the *savants* as a body, this ideal world threatens to take the place of a good God to the real world, reserving for its licensed representatives the office of priests. That is the reason why it is necessary to dissolve the special social organization of the *savants* by general instruction, equal for all in all things, in order that the masses, ceasing to be flocks led and shorn by privileged priests, may take into their own hands the direction of their destinies.*

But until the masses shall have reached this degree of instruction, will it be necessary to leave them to the government of scientific men? Certainly not. It would be better for them to dispense with science than allow themselves to be governed by *savants*. The first consequence of the government of these men would be to render science inaccessible to the people, and such a government would necessarily be aristocratic, because the existing scientific institutions are essentially aristocratic. An aristocracy of learning! from the practical point of view the most implacable, and from the social point of view the most haughty and insulting— such would be the power established in the name of science. This *régime* would be capable of paralyzing the life and movement of society. The *savants* always presumptuous, ever self-sufficient and ever impotent, would desire to meddle with everything, and the sources of life would dry up under the breath of their abstractions.

Once more, Life, not science, creates life; the spontane-

---

*Science, in becoming the patrimony of everybody, will wed itself in a certain sense to the immediate and real life of each. It will gain in utility and grace what it loses in pride, ambition, and *doctrinaire* pedantry. This, however, will not prevent men of genius, better organized for scientific speculation than the majority of their fellows, from devoting themselves exclusively to the cultivation of the sciences, and rendering great services to humanity. Only, they will be ambitious for no other social influence than the natural influence exercised upon its surroundings by every superior intelligence, and for no other reward than the high delight which a noble mind always finds in the satisfaction of a noble passion.

ous action of the people themselves alone can create liberty. Undoubtedly it would be a very fortunate thing if science could, from this day forth, illuminate the spontaneous march of the people towards their emancipation. But better an absence of light than a false and feeble light, kindled only to mislead those who follow it. After all, the people will not lack light. Not in vain have they traversed a long historic career, and paid for their errors by centuries of misery. The practical summary of their painful experiences constitutes a sort of traditional science, which in certain respects is worth as much as theoretical science. Last of all, a portion of the youth—those of the bourgeois students who feel hatred enough for the falsehood, hypocrisy, injustice, and cowardice of the bourgeoisie to find courage to turn their backs upon it, and passion enough to unreservedly embrace the just and human cause of the proletariat—those will be, as I have already said, fraternal instructors of the people; thanks to them, there will be no occasion for the government of the *savants*.

If the people should beware of the government of the *savants,* all the more should they provide against that of the inspired idealists. The more sincere these believers and poets of heaven, the more dangerous they become. The scientific abstraction, I have said, is a rational abstraction, true in its essence, necessary to life, of which it is the theoretical representation, or, if one prefers, the conscience. It may, it must be, absorbed and digested by life. The idealistic abstraction, God, is a corrosive poison, which destroys and decomposes life, falsifies and kills it. The pride of the idealists, not being personal but divine, is invincible and inexorable: it may, it must, die, but it will never yield, and while it has a breath left it will try to subject men to its God, just as the lieutenants of Prussia, these practical idealists of Germany, would like to see the people crushed under the spurred boot of their emperor. The faith is the same, the end but little different, and the result, as that of faith, is slavery.

It is at the same time the triumph of the ugliest and most brutal materialism. There is no need to demonstrate this in the case of Germany; one would have to be blind to avoid seeing it at the present hour. But I think it is still necessary to demonstrate it in the case of divine idealism.

Man, like all the rest of nature, is an entirely material being. The mind, the facility of thinking, of receiving and reflecting upon different external and internal sensations, of remembering them when they have passed and reproducing them by the imagination, of comparing and distinguishing them, of abstracting determinations common to them and thus creating general concepts, and finally of forming ideas by grouping and combining concepts according to different methods—intelligence, in a word, sole creator of our whole ideal world, is a property of the animal body and especially of the quite material organism of the brain.

We know this certainly, by the experience of all, which no fact has ever contradicted and which any man can verify at any moment of his life. In all animals, without excepting the wholly inferior species, we find a certain degree of intelligence, and we see that, in the series of species, animal intelligence develops in proportion as the organization of a species approaches that of man, but that in man alone it attains to that power of abstraction which properly constitutes thought.

Universal experience,* which is the sole origin, the source of all our knowledge, shows us, therefore, that all intelligence is always attached to some animal body, and that the intensity, the power, of this animal function depends upon the relative perfection of the organism. The latter of these results of universal experience is not applicable only to the different animal species; we establish it likewise in men,

---

*Universal *experience*, on which all science rests, must be clearly distinguished from universal *faith*, on which the idealists wish to support their beliefs: the first is a real authentication of facts; the second is only a supposition of facts which nobody has seen, and which consequently are at variance with the experience of everybody.

whose intellectual and moral power depends so clearly upon the greater or less perfection of their organism as a race, as a nation, as a class, and as individuals, that it is not necessary to insist upon this point.*

On the other hand, it is certain that no man has ever seen or can see pure mind, detached from all material form, existing separately from any animal body whatsoever. But if no person has seen it, how is it that men have come to believe in its existence? The fact of this belief is certain, and if not universal, as all the idealists pretend, at least very general, and as such it is entirely worthy of our closest attention, for a general belief, however foolish it may be, exercises too potent a sway over the destiny of men to warrant us in ignoring it or putting it aside.

The explanation of this belief, moreover, is rational enough. The example afforded us by children and young people, and even by many men long past the age of majority, shows us that man may use his mental faculties for a long time before accounting to himself for the way in which he uses them, before becoming clearly conscious of it. During this working of the mind unconscious of itself, during

---

*The idealists, all those who believe in the immateriality and immortality of the human soul, must be excessively embarrassed by the difference in intelligence existing between races, peoples, and individuals. Unless we suppose that the various divine particles have been irregularly distributed, how is this difference to be explained? Unfortunately there is a considerable number of men wholly stupid, foolish even to idiocy. Could they have received in the distribution a particle at once divine and stupid? To escape this embarrassment the idealists must necessarily suppose that all human souls are equal, but that the prisons in which they find themselves necessarily confined, human bodies, are unequal, some more capable than others of serving as an organ for the pure intellectuality of soul. According to this, such a one might have very fine organs at his disposition, such another very gross organs. But these are distinctions which idealism has not the power to use without falling into inconsistency and the grossest materialism; for in the presence of absolute immateriality of soul all bodily differences disappear, all that is corporeal, material, necessarily appearing

this action of innocent or believing intelligence, man, obsessed by the external world, pushed on by that internal goad called life and its manifold necessities, creates a quantity of imaginations, concepts, and ideas necessarily very imperfect at first and conforming but slightly to the reality of the things and facts which they endeavor to express. Not having yet the consciousness of his own intelligent action, not knowing yet that he himself has produced and continues to produce these imaginations, these concepts, these ideas, ignoring their wholly *subjective*—that is, human—origin, he must naturally consider them as *objective* beings, as real beings, wholly independent of him, existing by themselves and in themselves.

It was thus that primitive peoples, emerging slowly from their animal innocence, created their gods. Having created them, not suspecting that they themselves were the real creators, they worshipped them; considering them as real beings infinitely superior to themselves, they attributed omnipotence to them, and recognized themselves as their creatures, their slaves. As fast as human ideas develop, the gods, who, as I have already stated, were never anything more than a fantastic, ideal, poetical reverberation or an inverted image, become idealized also. At first gross fetiches,

indifferent, equally and absolutely gross. The abyss which separates soul from body, absolute immateriality from absolute materiality, is infinite. Consequently all differences, by the way inexplicable and logically impossible, which may exist on the other side of the abyss, in matter, should be to the soul null and void, and neither can nor should exercise any influence over it. In a word, the absolutely immaterial cannot be constrained, imprisoned, and much less expressed in any degree whatsoever by the absolutely material. Of all the gross and materialistic (using the word in the sense attached to it by the idealists) imaginations which were engendered by the primitive ignorance and stupidity of men, that of an immaterial soul imprisoned in a material body is certainly the grossest, the most stupid, and nothing better proves the omnipotence exercised by ancient prejudices even over the best minds than the deplorable sight of men endowed with lofty intelligence still talking of it in our days.

they gradually become pure spirits, existing outside of the visible world, and at last, in the course of a long historic evolution, are confounded in a single Divine Being, pure, eternal, absolute Spirit, creator and master of the worlds.

In every development, just or false, real or imaginary, collective or individual, it is always the first step, the first act that is the most difficult. That step once taken, the rest follows naturally as a necessary consequence. The difficult step in the historical development of this terrible religious insanity which continues to obsess and crush us was to posit a divine world as such, outside the world. This first act of madness, so natural from the physiological point of view and consequently necessary in the history of humanity, was not accomplished at a single stroke. I know not how many centuries were needed to develop this belief and make it a governing influence upon the mental customs of men. But, once established, it became omnipotent, as each insane notion necessarily becomes when it takes possession of man's brain. Take a madman, whatever the object of his madness —you will find that obscure and fixed idea which obsesses him seems to him the most natural thing in the world, and that, on the contrary, the real things which contradict this idea seem to him ridiculous and odious follies. Well, religion is a collective insanity, the more powerful because it is traditional folly, and because its origin is lost in the most remote antiquity. As collective insanity it has penetrated to the very depths of the public and private existence of the peoples; it is incarnate in society; it has become, so to speak, the collective soul and thought. Every man is enveloped in it from his birth; he sucks it in with his mother's milk, absorbs it with all that he touches, all that he sees. He is so exclusively fed upon it, so poisoned and penetrated by it in all his being, that later, however powerful his natural mind, he has to make unheard-of efforts to deliver himself from it, and even then never completely succeeds. We have one proof of this in our modern idealists, and another in our *doctrinaire* materialists—the German Communists.

They have found no way to shake off the religion of the State.

The supernatural world, the divine world, once well established in the imagination of the peoples, the development of the various religious systems has followed its natural and logical course, conforming, moreover, in all things to the contemporary development of economical and political relations of which it has been in all ages, in the world of religious fancy, the faithful reproduction and divine consecration. Thus has the collective and historical insanity which calls itself religion been developed since fetichism, passing through all the stages from polytheism to Christian monotheism.

The second step in the development of religious beliefs, undoubtedly the most difficult next to the establishment of a separate divine world, was precisely this transition from polytheism to monotheism, from the religious materialism of the pagans to the spiritualistic faith of the Christians. The pagan gods—and this was their principal characteristic —were first of all exclusively national gods. Very numerous, they necessarily retained a more or less material character, or, rather, they were so numerous because they were material, diversity being one of the principal attributes of the real world. The pagan gods were not yet strictly the negation of real things; they were only a fantastic exaggeration of them.

We have seen how much this transition cost the Jewish people, constituting, so to speak, its entire history. In vain did Moses and the prophets preach the one god; the people always relapsed into their primitive idolatry, into the ancient and comparatively much more natural and convenient faith in many good gods, more material, more human, and more palpable. Jehovah himself, their sole God, the God of Moses and the prophets, was still an extremely national God, who, to reward and punish his faithful followers, his chosen people, used material arguments, often stupid, always gross and cruel. It does not even appear that faith in his existence implied a negation of the existence of earlier gods. The Jewish God did not deny the existence of these rivals; he simply did not want his people to worship them side by side with him, because before all Jehovah was a very jealous God. His first commandment was this:

"I am the Lord thy God, and thou shalt have no other gods before me."

Jehovah, then, was only a first draft, very material and very rough, of the supreme deity of modern idealism. Moreover, he was only a national God, like the Russian God worshipped by the German generals, subjects of the Czar and patriots of the empire of all the Russias; like the German God, whom the pietists and the German generals, subjects of William I. at Berlin, will no doubt soon proclaim. The supreme being cannot be a national God; he must be the God of entire Humanity. Nor can the supreme being be a material being; he must be the negation of all matter— pure spirit. Two things have proved necessary to the realization of the worship of the supreme being: (1) a realization, such as it is, of Humanity by the negation of nationalities and national forms of worship; (2) a development, already far advanced, of metaphysical ideas in order to spiritualize the gross Jehovah of the Jews.

The first condition was fulfilled by the Romans, though in a very negative way no doubt, by the conquest of most of the countries known to the ancients and by the destruction of their national institutions. The gods of all the conquered nations, gathered in the Pantheon, mutually cancelled each other. This was the first draft of humanity, very gross and quite negative.

As for the second condition, the spiritualization of Jehovah, that was realized by the Greeks long before the conquest of their country by the Romans. They were the creators of metaphysics. Greece, in the cradle of her history, had already found from the Orient a divine world which had been definitely established in the traditional faith of her peoples; this world had been left and handed over to her by the Orient. In her instinctive period, prior to her political history, she had developed and prodigiously humanized this divine world through her poets; and when she actually began her history, she already had a religion ready-made, the most sympathetic and noble of all the religions which have existed, so far at least as a religion—that is, a lie—can be noble and sympathetic. Her great thinkers—and no nation has had greater than Greece—found the divine world established, not only outside of themselves in the people, but also in themselves as a habit of feeling and thought, and naturally they took it as a point of departure. That they made no theology—that is, that they did not wait in vain to reconcile dawning reason with the absurdities of such a god, as did the scholastics of the Middle Ages—was already much in their favor. They left the gods out of their speculations and attached themselves directly to the divine idea, one, invisible, omnipotent, eternal, and absolutely spiritualistic but impersonal. As concerns Spiritualism, then, the Greek metaphysicians, much more than the Jews, were the creators of the Christian god. The Jews only added to it the brutal personality of their Jehovah.

That a sublime genius like the divine Plato could have been absolutely convinced of the reality of the divine idea shows us how contagious, how omnipotent, is the tradition of the religious mania even on the greatest minds. Besides, we should not be surprised at it, since, even in our day, the greatest philosophical genius which has existed since Aristotle and Plato, Hegel—in spite even of Kant's criticism, imperfect and too metaphysical though it be, which had demolished the objectivity or reality of the divine ideas—tried to replace these divine ideas upon their transcendental or celestial throne. It is true that Hegel went about his work of restoration in so impolite a manner that he killed the good God for ever. He took away from these ideas their divine halo, by showing to whoever will read him that they were never anything more than a creation of the human mind running through history in search of itself. To put an end to all religious insanities and the divine *mirage,* he left nothing lacking but the utterance of those grand words which were said after him, almost at the same time, by two great minds who had never heard of each other —Ludwig Feuerbach, the disciple and demolisher of Hegel, in Germany, and Auguste Comte, the founder of positive philosophy, in France. These words were as follows:

"Metaphysics are reduced to psychology." All the metaphysical systems have been nothing else than human psychology developing itself in history.

To-day it is no longer difficult to understand how the divine ideas were born, how they were created in succession by the abstractive faculty of man. Man made the gods. But in the time of Plato this knowledge was impossible. The collective mind, and consequently the individual mind as well, even that of the greatest genius, was not ripe for that. Scarcely had it said with Socrates: "Know thyself!" This self-knowledge existed only in a state of intuition; in fact, it amounted to nothing. Hence it was impossible for the human mind to suspect that it was itself the sole creator of the divine world. It found the divine world before it; it found it as history, as tradition, as a sentiment, as a habit of thought; and it necessarily made it the object of its loftiest speculations. Thus was born metaphysics, and thus were developed and perfected the divine ideas, the basis of Spiritualism.

It is true that after Plato there was a sort of inverse movement in the development of the mind. Aristotle, the true father of science and positive philosophy, did not deny the divine world, but concerned himself with it as little as possible. He was the first to study, like the analyst and experimenter that he was, logic, the laws of human thought, and at the same time the physical world, not in its ideal, illusory essence, but in its real aspect. After him the Greeks of Alexandria established the first school of the positive scientists. They were atheists. But their atheism left no mark on their contemporaries. Science tended more and

more to separate itself from life. After Plato, divine ideas
were rejected in metaphysics themselves; this was done by
the Epicureans and Skeptics, two sects who contributed
much to the degradation of human aristocracy, but they had
no effect upon the masses.

Another school, infinitely more influential, was formed
at Alexandria. This was the school of neo-Platonists.
These, confounding in an impure mixture the monstrous
imaginations of the Orient with the ideas of Plato, were
the true originators, and later the elaborators, of the Christian dogmas.

Thus the personal and gross egoism of Jehovah, the not
less brutal and gross Roman conquest, and the metaphysical
ideal speculation of the Greeks, materialized by contact with
the Orient, were the three historical elements which made
up the spiritualistic religion of the Christians.

Before the altar of a unique and supreme God was
raised on the ruins of the numerous altars of the pagan gods,
the autonomy of the various nations composing the pagan
or ancient world had to be destroyed first. This was very
brutally done by the Romans who, by conquering the greatest part of the globe known to the ancients, laid the first
foundations, quite gross and negative ones no doubt, of humanity. A God thus raised above the national differences,
material and social, of all countries, and in a certain sense
the direct negation of them, must necessarily be an immaterial and abstract being. But faith in the existence of such
a being, so difficult a matter, could not spring into existence
suddenly. Consequently, as I have demonstrated in the
Appendix, it went through a long course of preparation and
development at the hands of Greek metaphysics, which were
the first to establish in a philosophical manner the notion of
the divine idea, a model eternally creative and always reproduced by the visible world. But the divinity conceived and
created by Greek philosophy was an impersonal divinity.
No logical and serious metaphysics being able to rise, or,

rather, to descend, to the idea of a personal God, it became necessary, therefore, to imagine a God who was one and very personal at once. He was found in the very brutal, selfish, and cruel person of Jehovah, the national God of the Jews. But the Jews, in spite of that exclusive national spirit which distinguishes them even to-day, had become in fact, long before the birth of Christ, the most international people of the world. Some of them carried away as captives, but many more even urged on by that mercantile passion which constitutes one of the principal traits of their character, they had spread through all countries, carrying everywhere the worship of their Jehovah, to whom they remained all the more faithful the more he abandoned them.

In Alexandria this terrible god of the Jews made the personal acquaintance of the metaphysical divinity of Plato, already much corrupted by Oriental contact, and corrupted her still more by his own. In spite of his national, jealous, and ferocious exclusivism, he could not long resist the graces of this ideal and impersonal divinity of the Greeks. He married her, and from this marriage was born the spiritualistic—but not spirited—God of the Christians. The neo-Platonists of Alexandria are known to have been the principal creators of the Christian theology.

Nevertheless theology alone does not make a religion, any more than historical elements suffice to create history. By historical elements I mean the general conditions of any real development whatsoever—for example in this case the conquest of the world by the Romans and the meeting of the God of the Jews with the ideal of divinity of the Greeks. To impregnate the historical elements, to cause them to run through a series of new historical transformations, a living, spontaneous fact was needed, without which they might have remained many centuries longer in the state of unproductive elements. This fact was not lacking in Christianity: it was the propagandism, martyrdom, and death of Jesus Christ.

We know almost nothing of this great and saintly personage, all that the gospels tell us being contradictory, and so fabulous that we can scarcely seize upon a few real and vital traits. But it is certain that he was the preacher of the poor, the friend and consoler of the wretched, of the ignorant, of the slaves, and of the women, and that by these last he was much loved. He promised eternal life to all who are oppressed, to all who suffer here below; and the number is immense. He was hanged, as a matter of course, by the representatives of the official morality and public order of that period. His disciples and the disciples of his disciples succeeded in spreading, thanks to the destruction of the national barriers by the Roman conquest, and propagated the Gospel in all the countries known to the ancients. Everywhere they were received with open arms by the slaves and the women, the two most oppressed, most suffering, and naturally also the most ignorant classes of the ancient world. For even such few proselytes as they made in the privileged and learned world they were indebted in great part to the influence of women. Their most extensive propagandism was directed almost exclusively among the people, unfortunate and degraded by slavery. This was the first awakening, the first intellectual revolt of the proletariat.

The great honor of Christianity, its incontestable merit, and the whole secret of its unprecedented and yet thoroughly legitimate triumph, lay in the fact that it appealed to that suffering and immense public to which the ancient world, a strict and cruel intellectual and political aristocracy, denied even the simplest rights of humanity. Otherwise it never could have spread. The doctrine taught by the apostles of Christ, wholly consoling as it may have seemed to the unfortunate, was too revolting, too absurd from the standpoint of human reason, ever to have been accepted by enlightened men. According with what joy the apostle Paul speaks of the *scandale de la foi* and of the triumph of that *divine folie* rejected by the powerful and wise of the

century, but all the more passionately accepted by the simple,
the ignorant, and the weak-minded!

Indeed there must have been a very deep-seated dissatis-
faction with life, a very intense thirst of heart, and an almost absolute poverty of thought, to secure the acceptance
of the Christian absurdity, the most audacious and monstrous of all religious absurdities.

This was not only the negation of all the political, social,
and religious institutions of antiquity: it was the absolute
overturn of common sense, of all human reason. The living
being, the real world, were considered thereafter as nothing;
whereas the product of man's abstractive faculty, the last
and supreme abstraction in which this faculty, far beyond
existing things, even beyond the most general determinations
of the living being, the ideas of space and time, having nothing left to advance beyond, rests in contemplation of his
emptiness and absolute immobility.

That abstraction, that *caput mortuum,* absolutely void of
all contents, the true nothing, God. is proclaimed the only
real, eternal, all-powerful being. The real All is declared
nothing, and the absolute nothing the All. The shadow becomes the substance, and the substance vanishes like a
shadow.*

All this was audacity and absurdity unspeakable, the
true *scandale de la foi,* the triumph of credulous stupidity
over the mind for the masses; and—for a few—the triumphant irony of a mind wearied, corrupted, disillusioned,
and disgusted in honest and serious search for truth; it was

---

*I am well aware that in the theological and metaphysical sys-
tems of the Orient, and especially in those of India, including
Buddhism, we find the principle of the annihilation of the real
world in favor of the ideal and of absolute abstraction. But it has
not the added character of voluntary and deliberate negation which
distinguishes Christianity; when those systems were conceived, the
world of human thought, of will and of liberty, had not reached
that stage of development which was afterwards seen in the Greek
and Roman civilization.

that necessity of shaking off thought and becoming brutally stupid so frequently felt by surfeited minds:

Credo quod absurdum.

I believe in the absurd; I believe in it, precisely and mainly, because it is absurd. In the same way many distinguished and enlightened minds in our day believe in animal magnetism, spiritualism, tipping tables, and—why go so far?—believe still in Christianity, in idealism, in God.

The belief of the ancient proletariat, like that of the modern, was more robust and simple, less *haut goût*. The Christian propagandism appealed to its heart, not to its mind; to its eternal aspirations, its necessities, its sufferings, its slavery, not to its reason, which still slept and therefore could know nothing about logical contradictions and the evidence of the absurd. It was interested solely in knowing when the hour of promised deliverance would strike, when the kingdom of God would come. As for theological dogmas, it did not trouble itself about them because it understood nothing about them. The proletariat converted to Christianity constituted its growing material but not its intellectual strength.

As for the Christian dogmas, it is known that they were elaborated in a series of theological and literary works and in the Councils, principally by the converted neo-Platonists of the Orient. The Greek mind had fallen so low that, in the fourth century of the Christian era, the period of the first Council, the idea of a personal God, pure, eternal, absolute mind, creator and supreme master, existing outside of the world, was unanimously accepted by the Church Fathers; as a logical consequence of this absolute absurdity, it then became natural and necessary to believe in the immateriality and immortality of the human soul, lodged and imprisoned in a body only partially mortal, there being in this body itself a portion which, while material, is immortal like the soul, and must be resurrected with it. We see how difficult it was, even for the Church Fathers, to conceive pure minds outside of any material form. It should be added that, in general, it is the character of every meta-physical and theological argument to seek to explain one absurdity by another.

It was very fortunate for Christianity that it met a world of slaves. It had another piece of good luck in the invasion of the Barbarians. The latter were worthy people, full of natural force, and, above all, urged on by a great necessity of life and a great capacity for it; brigands who had stood every test, capable of devastating and gobbling up anything, like their successors, the Germans of to-day; but they were much less systematic and pedantic than these last, much less moralistic, less learned, and on the other hand much more independent and proud, capable of science and not incapable of liberty, as are the bourgeois of modern Germany. But, in spite of all their great qualities, they were nothing but barbarians—that is, as indifferent to all questions of theology and metaphysics as the ancient slaves, a great number of whom, moreover, belonged to their race. So that, their practical repugnance once overcome, it was not difficult to convert them theoretically to Christianity.

For ten centuries Christianity, armed with the omni-potence of Church and State and opposed by no competition, was able to deprave, debase, and falsify the mind of Europe. It had no competitors, because outside of the Church there were neither thinkers nor educated persons. It alone thought, it alone spoke and wrote, it alone taught. Though heresies arose in its bosom, they affected only the theologi-cal or practical developments of the fundamental dogma, never that dogma itself. The belief in God, pure spirit and creator of the world, and the belief in the immateriality of the soul remained untouched. This double belief became the ideal basis of the whole Occidental and Oriental civil-ization of Europe; it penetrated and became incarnate in all the institutions, all the details of the public and private life of all classes, and the masses as well.

After that, is it surprising that this belief has lived until

the present day, continuing to exercise its disastrous influence even upon select minds, such as those of Mazzini,
Michelet, Quinet, and so many others? We have seen that
the first attack upon it came from the *renaissance* of the
free mind in the fifteenth century, which produced heroes
and martyrs like Vanini, Giordano Bruno, and Galileo. Although drowned in the noise, tumult, and passions of the
Reformation, it noiselessly continued its invisible work, be-
queathing to the noblest minds of each generation its task
of human emancipation by the destruction of the absurd,
until at last, in the latter half of the eighteenth century, it
again reappeared in broad day, boldly waving the flag of
atheism and materialism.

The human mind, then, one might have supposed, was
at last about to deliver itself from all the divine obsessions.
Not at all. The divine falsehood upon which humanity had
been feeding for eighteen centuries (speaking of Christianity only) was once more to show itself more powerful than
human truth. No longer able to make use of the black
tribe, of the ravens consecrated by the Church, of the Catholic or Protestant priests, all confidence in whom had been
lost, it made use of lay priests, short-robed liars and sophists.
among whom the principal *rôles* devolved upon two fatal
men, one the falsest mind, the other the most doctrinally
despotic will, of the last century—J. J. Rousseau and Robespierre.

The first is the perfect type of narrowness and suspi-
cious meanness, of exaltation without other object than his
own person, of cold enthusiasm and hypocrisy at once sentimental and implacable, of the falsehood of modern idealism. He may be considered as the real creator of modern
reaction. To all appearance the most democratic writer of
the eighteenth century, he bred within himself the pitiless
despotism of the statesman. He was the prophet of the doctrinaire State, as Robespierre, his worthy and faithful disciple, tried to become its high priest. Having heard the
saying of Voltaire that, if God did not exist, it would be

necessary to invent him, J. J. Rousseau invented the Supreme Being, the abstract and sterile God of the deists. And it was in the name of the Supreme Being, and of the hypocritical virtue commanded by this Supreme Being, that Robespierre guillotined first the Hébertists and then the very genius of the Revolution, Danton, in whose person he assassinated the Republic, thus preparing the way for the thenceforth necessary triumph of the dictatorship of Bonaparte I. After this great triumph, the idealistic reaction sought and found servants less fanatical, less terrible, nearer to the diminished stature of the actual bourgeoisie. In France, Chateaubriand, Lamartine, and—shall I say it? Why not? All must be said if it is truth—Victor Hugo himself, the democrat, the republican, the quasi-socialist of today! and after them the whole melancholy and sentimental company of poor and pallid minds who, under the leadership of these masters, established the modern romantic school; in Germany, the Schlegels, the Tiecks, the Novalis, the Werners, the Schellings, and so many others besides, whose names do not even deserve to be recalled.

The literature created by this school was the very reign of ghosts and phantoms. It could not stand the sunlight; the twilight alone permitted it to live. No more could it stand the brutal contact of the masses. It was the literature of the tender, delicate, distinguished souls, aspiring to heaven, and living on earth as if in spite of themselves. It had a horror and contempt for the politics and questions of the day; but when perchance it referred to them, it showed itself frankly reactionary, took the side of the Church against the insolence of the freethinkers, of the kings against the peoples, and of all the aristocrats against the vile rabble of the streets. For the rest, as I have just said, the dominant feature of the school of romanticism was a quasi-complete indifference to politics. Amid the clouds in which it lived could be distinguished two real points— the rapid development of bourgeois materialism and the ungovernable outburst of individual vanities.

To understand this romantic literature, the reason for its existence must be sought in the transformation which had been effected in the bosom of the bourgeois class since the revolution of 1793.

From the Renaissance and the Reformation down to the Revolution, the bourgeoisie, if not in Germany, at least in Italy, in France, in Switzerland, in England, in Holland, was the hero and representative of the revolutionary genius of history. From its bosom sprang most of the freethinkers of the fifteenth century, the religious reformers of the two following centuries, and the apostles of human emancipation, including this time those of Germany, of the past century. It alone, naturally supported by the powerful arm of the people, who had faith in it, made the revolution of 1789 and '93. It proclaimed the downfall of royalty and of the Church, the fraternity of the peoples, the rights of man and of the citizen. Those are its titles to glory; they are immortal!

Soon it split. A considerable portion of the purchasers of national property having become rich, and supporting themselves no longer on the proletariat of the cities, but on the major portion of the peasants of France, these also having become landed proprietors, had no aspiration left but for peace, the re-establishment of public order, and the foundation of a strong and regular government. It therefore welcomed with joy the dictatorship of the first Bonaparte, and, although always Voltairean, did not view with displeasure the Concordat with the Pope and the re-establishment of the official Church in France: *"Religion is so necessary to the people!"* Which means that, satiated themselves, this portion of the bourgeoisie then began to see that it was needful to the maintenance of their situation and the preservation of their newly-acquired estates to appease the unsatisfied hunger of the people by promises of heavenly manna. Then it was that Chateaubriand began to preach.*

---

*It seems to me useful to recall at this point an anecdote—one, by the way, well known and thoroughly authentic—which sheds

Napoleon fell and the Restoration brought back into France the legitimate monarchy, and with it the power of the Church and of the nobles, who regained, if not the whole, at least a considerable portion of their former influence. This reaction threw the bourgeoisie back into the Revolution, and with the revolutionary spirit that of skepticism also was re-awakened in it. It set Chateaubriand aside and began to read Voltaire again; but it did not go so far as Diderot: its debilitated nerves could not stand nourishment so strong. Voltaire, on the contrary, at once a freethinker and a deist, suited it very well. Béranger and P. L. Courier expressed this new tendency perfectly. The "God of the good people" and the ideal of the bourgeois king, at once liberal and democratic, sketched against the majestic and thenceforth inoffensive background of the Empire's gigantic victories—such was at that period the daily intellectual food of the bourgeoisie of France.

Lamartine, to be sure, excited by a vain and ridiculously envious desire to rise to the poetic height of the great Byron, had begun his coldly delirious hymns in honor of the God of the nobles and of the legitimate monarchy. But his songs resounded only in aristocratic salons. The bourgeoisie did not hear them. Béranger was its poet and Courier was its political writer.

The revolution of July resulted in lifting its tastes. We know that every bourgeois in France carries within him the imperishable type of the bourgeois gentleman, a type which never fails to appear immediately the parvenu acquires a little wealth and power. In 1830 the wealthy bourgeoisie had definitely replaced the old nobility in the seats of power.

---

a very clear light on the personal value of this warmer-over of the Catholic beliefs and on the religious sincerity of that period. Chateaubriand submitted to a publisher a work attacking faith. The publisher called his attention to the fact that atheism had gone out of fashion, that the reading public cared no more for it, and that the demand, on the contrary, was for religious works. Chateaubriand withdrew, but a few months later came back with his *Genius of Christianity*.

GOD AND THE STATE

It naturally tended to establish a new aristocracy. An aristocracy of capital first of all, but also an aristocracy of intellect, of good manners and delicate sentiments. It began to feel religious.

This was not on its part simply an aping of aristocratic customs. It was also a necessity of its position. The proletariat had rendered it a final service in once more aiding it to overthrow the nobility. The bourgeoisie now had no further need of its co-operation, for it felt itself firmly seated in the shadow of the throne of July, and the alliance with the people, thenceforth useless, began to become inconvenient. It was necessary to remand it to its place, which naturally could not be done without provoking great indignation among the masses. It became necessary to restrain this indignation. In the name of what? In the name of the bourgeois interest bluntly confessed? That would have been much too cynical. The more unjust and inhuman an interest is, the greater need it has of sanction. Now, where find it if not in religion, that good protectress of all the well-fed and the useful consoler of the hungry? And more than ever the triumphant burgeoisie saw that religion was indispensable to the people.

After having won all its titles to glory in religious, philosophical, and political opposition, in protest and in revolution, it at last became the dominant class and thereby even the defender and preserver of the State, thenceforth the regular institution of the exclusive power of that class. The State is force, and for it, first of all, is the right of force, the triumphant argument of the needle-gun, of the *chassepot*. But man is so singuarly constituted that this argument, wholly eloquent as it may appear, is not sufficient in the long run. Some moral sanction or other is absolutely necessary to enforce his respect. Further, this sanction must be at once so simple and so plain that it may convince the masses, who, after having been reduced by the power of the State, must also be induced to morally recognize its right.

There are only two ways of convincing the masses of the goodness of any social institution whatever. The first, the only real one, but also the most difficult to adopt—because it implies the abolition of the State, or, in other words, the abolition of the organized political exploitation of the majority by any minority whatsoever—would be the direct and complete satisfaction of the needs and aspirations of the people, which would be equivalent to the complete liquidation of the political and economical existence of the bourgeois class, or, again, to the abolition of the State. Beneficial means for the masses, but detrimental to bourgeois interests; hence it is useless to talk about them.

The only way, on the contrary, harmful only to the people, precious in its salvation of bourgeois privileges, is no other than religion. That is the eternal *mirage* which leads away the masses in a search for divine treasures, while, much more reserved, the governing class contents itself with dividing among all its members—very unequally, moreover, and always giving most to him who possesses most—the miserable goods of earth and the plunder taken from the people, including their political and social liberty.

There is not, there cannot be, a State without religion. Take the freest States in the world—the United States of America or the Swiss Confederation, for instance—and see what an important part is played in all official discourses by divine Providence, that supreme sanction of all States.

But whenever a chief of State speaks of God, be he William I., the Knouto-Germanic emperor, or Grant, the president of the great republic, be sure that he is getting ready to shear once more his people-flock.

The French liberal and Voltairean bourgeoisie, driven by temperament to a positivism (not to say a materialism) singularly narrow and brutal, having become the governing class of the State by its triumph of 1830, had to give itself an official religion. It was not an easy thing. The bourgeoisie could not abruptly go back under the yoke of Roman Catholicism. Between it and the Church of Rome was an abyss of blood and hatred, and, however practical and wise one becomes, it is never possible to repress a passion developed by history. Moreover, the French bourgeoisie would have covered itself with ridicule if it had gone back to the Church to take part in the pious ceremonies of its worship, an essential condition of a meretorious and sincere conversion. Several attempted it, it is true, but their heroism was rewarded by no other result than a fruitless scandal. Finally, a return to Catholicism was impossible on account of the insolvable contradiction which separates the invariable politics of Rome from the development of the economical and political interests of the middle class.

In this respect Protestantism is much more advantageous. It is the bourgeois religion *par excellence*. It accords just as much liberty as is necessary to the bourgeois, and finds a way of reconciling celestial aspirations with the respect which terrestrial conditions demand. Consequently it is especially in Protestant countries that commerce and industry have been developed. But it was impossible for the French bourgeoisie to become Protestant. To pass from one religion to another—unless it be done deliberately, as sometimes in the case of the Jews of Russia and Poland, who get baptised three or four times in order to receive each time the remuneration allowed them—to seriously change one's religion, a little faith is necessary. Now, in the exclusive positive heart of the French bourgeois, there is no room for faith. He professes the most profound indifference for all questions which touch neither his pocket first nor his social vanity afterwards. He is as indifferent to Protestantism as to Catholicism. On the other hand, the French bourgeois could not go over to Protestantism without putting himself in conflict with the Catholic routine of the majority of the French people, which would have been great imprudence on the part of a class pretending to govern the nation.

There was still one way left—to return to the humanitarian and revolutionary religion of the eighteenth century. But that would have led too far. So the bourgeoisie was obliged, in order to sanction its new State, to create a new religion which might be boldly proclaimed, without too much ridicule and scandal, by the whole bourgeois class.

Thus was born *doctrinaire* Deism.

Others have told, much better than I could tell it, the story of the birth and development of this school, which had so decisive and—we may well add—so fatal an influence on the political, intellectual, and moral education of the bourgeois youth of France. It dates from Benjamin Constant and Madame de Staël; its real founder was Royer-Collard; its apostles, Guizot, Cousin, Villemain, and many others. Its boldly avowed object was the reconciliation of Revolution with Reaction, or, to use the language of the school, of the principle of liberty with that of authority, and naturally to the advantage of the latter.

This reconciliation signified: in politics, the taking away of popular liberty for the benefit of bourgeois rule, represented by the monarchical and constitutional State; in philosophy, the deliberate submission of free reason to the eternal principles of faith. We have only to deal here with the latter.

We know that this philosophy was specially elaborated by M. Cousin, the father of French eclecticism. A superficial and pedantic talker, incapable of any original conception, of any idea peculiar to himself, but very strong on commonplace, which he confounded with common sense, this illustrious philosopher learnedly prepared, for the use of the studious youth of France, a metaphysical dish of his own making, the use of which, made compulsory in all schools of the State under the University, condemned several generations one after the other to a cerebral indigestion. Imagine a philosophical vinegar sauce of the most opposed systems, a mixture of Fathers of the Church, scholastic philosophers, Descartes and Pascal, Kant and Scotch psychologists, all this a superstructure on the divine and innate ideas of Plato, and covered up with a layer of Hegelian immanence, accompanied, of course, by an ignorance, as contemptuous as it is complete, of natural science, and proving, just as two times two make *five*, the existence of a personal God. . . . .

INDEX OF PERSONS

A CATALOGUE OF SELECTED DOVER BOOKS
IN ALL FIELDS OF INTEREST

A CATALOGUE OF SELECTED DOVER BOOKS IN ALL FIELDS OF INTEREST

CELESTIAL OBJECTS FOR COMMON TELESCOPES, T. W. Webb. The most used book in amateur astronomy: inestimable aid for locating and identifying nearly 4,000 celestial objects. Edited, updated by Margaret W. Mayall. 77 illustrations. Total of 645pp. 5⅜ x 8½.
20917-2, 20918-0 Pa., Two-vol. set $9.00

HISTORICAL STUDIES IN THE LANGUAGE OF CHEMISTRY, M. P. Crosland. The important part language has played in the development of chemistry from the symbolism of alchemy to the adoption of systematic nomenclature in 1892. ". . . wholeheartedly recommended,"—Science. 15 illustrations. 416pp. of text. 5⅝ x 8¼.
63702-6 Pa. $6.00

BURNHAM'S CELESTIAL HANDBOOK, Robert Burnham, Jr. Thorough, readable guide to the stars beyond our solar system. Exhaustive treatment, fully illustrated. Breakdown is alphabetical by constellation: Andromeda to Cetus in Vol. 1; Chamaeleon to Orion in Vol. 2; and Pavo to Vulpecula in Vol. 3. Hundreds of illustrations. Total of about 2000pp. 6⅛ x 9¼.
23567-X, 23568-8, 23673-0 Pa., Three-vol. set $26.85

THEORY OF WING SECTIONS: INCLUDING A SUMMARY OF AIR-FOIL DATA, Ira H. Abbott and A. E. von Doenhoff. Concise compilation of subatomic aerodynamic characteristics of modern NASA wing sections, plus description of theory. 350pp. of tables. 693pp. 5⅜ x 8½.
60586-8 Pa. $7.00

DE RE METALLICA, Georgius Agricola. Translated by Herbert C. Hoover and Lou H. Hoover. The famous Hoover translation of greatest treatise on technological chemistry, engineering, geology, mining of early modern times (1556). All 289 original woodcuts. 638pp. 6¾ x 11.
60006-8 Clothbd. $17.95

THE ORIGIN OF CONTINENTS AND OCEANS, Alfred Wegener. One of the most influential, most controversial books in science, the classic statement for continental drift. Full 1966 translation of Wegener's final (1929) version. 64 illustrations. 246pp. 5⅜ x 8½. 61708-4 Pa. $4.50

THE PRINCIPLES OF PSYCHOLOGY, William James. Famous long course complete, unabridged. Stream of thought, time perception, memory, experimental methods; great work decades ahead of its time. Still valid, useful; read in many classes. 94 figures. Total of 1391pp. 5⅜ x 8½.
20381-6, 20382-4 Pa., Two-vol. set $13.00

A MAYA GRAMMAR, Alfred M. Tozzer. Practical, useful English-language grammar by the Harvard anthropologist who was one of the three greatest American scholars in the area of Maya culture. Phonetics, grammatical processes, syntax, more. 301pp. 5⅜ x 8½.   23465-7 Pa. $4.00

THE JOURNAL OF HENRY D. THOREAU, edited by Bradford Torrey, F. H. Allen. Complete reprinting of 14 volumes, 1837-61, over two million words; the sourcebooks for Walden, etc. Definitive. All original sketches, plus 75 photographs. Introduction by Walter Harding. Total of 1804pp. 8½ x 12¼.   20312-3, 20313-1 Clothbd., Two-vol. set $50.00

CLASSIC GHOST STORIES, Charles Dickens and others. 18 wonderful stories you've wanted to reread: "The Monkey's Paw," "The House and the Brain," "The Upper Berth," "The Signalman," "Dracula's Guest," "The Tapestried Chamber," etc. Dickens, Scott, Mary Shelley, Stoker, etc. 330pp. 5⅜ x 8½.   20735-8 Pa. $3.50

SEVEN SCIENCE FICTION NOVELS, H. G. Wells. Full novels. First Men in the Moon, Island of Dr. Moreau, War of the Worlds, Food of the Gods, Invisible Man, Time Machine, In the Days of the Comet. A basic science-fiction library. 1015pp. 5⅜ x 8½. (Available in U.S. only)
                20264-X Clothbd. $8.95

ARMADALE, Wilkie Collins. Third great mystery novel by the author of The Woman in White and The Moonstone. Ingeniously plotted narrative shows an exceptional command of character, incident and mood. Original magazine version with 40 illustrations. 597pp. 5⅜ x 8½.
                23429-0 Pa. $5.00

MASTERS OF MYSTERY, H. Douglas Thomson. The first book in English (1931) devoted to history and aesthetics of detective story. Poe, Doyle, LeFanu, Dickens, many others, up to 1930. New introduction and notes by E. F. Bleiler. 288pp. 5⅜ x 8½. (Available in U.S. only)
                23606-4 Pa. $4.00

FLATLAND, E. A. Abbott. Science-fiction classic explores life of 2-D being in 3-D world. Read also as introduction to thought about hyperspace. Introduction by Banesh Hoffmann. 16 illustrations. 103pp. 5⅜ x 8½.
                20001-9 Pa. $1.75

THREE SUPERNATURAL NOVELS OF THE VICTORIAN PERIOD, edited, with an introduction, by E. F. Bleiler. Reprinted complete and unabridged, three great classics of the supernatural: The Haunted Hotel by Wilkie Collins, The Haunted House at Latchford by Mrs. J. H. Riddell, and The Lost Stradivarius by J. Meade Falkner. 325pp. 5⅜ x 8½.
                22571-2 Pa. $4.00

AYESHA: THE RETURN OF "SHE," H. Rider Haggard. Virtuoso sequel featuring the great mythic creation, Ayesha, in an adventure that is fully as good as the first book, She. Original magazine version, with 47 original illustrations by Maurice Greiffenhagen. 189pp. 6½ x 9¼.
                23649-8 Pa. $3.50

AMERICAN BIRD ENGRAVINGS, Alexander Wilson et al. All 76 plates. from Wilson's *American Ornithology* (1808-14), most important ornithological work before Audubon, plus 27 plates from the supplement (1825-33) by Charles Bonaparte. Over 250 birds portrayed. 8 plates also reproduced in full color. 111pp. 9⅜ x 12½.

23195-X Pa. $6.00

CRUICKSHANK'S PHOTOGRAPHS OF BIRDS OF AMERICA, Allan D. Cruickshank. Great ornithologist, photographer presents 177 closeups, groupings, panoramas, flightings, etc., of about 150 different birds. Expanded *Wings in the Wilderness*. Introduction by Helen G. Cruickshank. 191pp. 8¼ x 11.

23497-5 Pa. $6.00

AMERICAN WILDLIFE AND PLANTS, A. C. Martin, et al. Describes food habits of more than 1000 species of mammals, birds, fish. Special treatment of important food plants. Over 300 illustrations. 500pp. 5⅜ x 8½.

20793-5 Pa. $4.95

THE PEOPLE CALLED SHAKERS, Edward D. Andrews. Lifetime of research, definitive study of Shakers: origins, beliefs, practices, dances, social organization, furniture and crafts, impact on 19th-century USA, present heritage. Indispensable to student of American history, collector. 33 illustrations. 351pp. 5⅜ x 8½.

21081-2 Pa. $4.00

OLD NEW YORK IN EARLY PHOTOGRAPHS, Mary Black. New York City as it was in 1853-1901, through 196 wonderful photographs from N.-Y. Historical Society. Great Blizzard, Lincoln's funeral procession, great buildings. 228pp. 9 x 12.

22907-6 Pa. $7.95

MR. LINCOLN'S CAMERA MAN: MATHEW BRADY, Roy Meredith. Over 300 Brady photos reproduced directly from original negatives, photos. Jackson, Webster, Grant, Lee, Carnegie, Barnum; Lincoln; Battle Smoke, Death of Rebel Sniper, Atlanta Just After Capture. Lively commentary. 368pp. 8⅜ x 11¼.

23021-X Pa. $8.95

TRAVELS OF WILLIAM BARTRAM, William Bartram. From 1773-8, Bartram explored Northern Florida, Georgia, Carolinas, and reported on wild life, plants, Indians, early settlers. Basic account for period, entertaining reading. Edited by Mark Van Doren. 13 illustrations. 141pp. 5⅜ x 8½.

20013-2 Pa. $4.50

THE GENTLEMAN AND CABINET MAKER'S DIRECTOR, Thomas Chippendale. Full reprint, 1762 style book, most influential of all time; chairs, tables, sofas, mirrors, cabinets, etc. 200 plates, plus 24 photographs of surviving pieces. 249pp. 9⅞ x 12¾.

21601-2 Pa. $6.50

AMERICAN CARRIAGES, SLEIGHS, SULKIES AND CARTS, edited by Don H. Berkebile. 168 Victorian illustrations from catalogues, trade journals, fully captioned. Useful for artists. Author is Assoc. Curator, Div. of Transportation of Smithsonian Institution. 168pp. 8½ x 9½.

23328-6 Pa. $5.00

AN AUTOBIOGRAPHY, Margaret Sanger. Exciting personal account of hard-fought battle for woman's right to birth control, against prejudice, church, law. Foremost feminist document. 504pp. 5⅜ x 8½.
20470-7 Pa. $5.50

MY BONDAGE AND MY FREEDOM, Frederick Douglass. Born as a slave, Douglass became outspoken force in antislavery movement. The best of Douglass's autobiographies. Graphic description of slave life. Introduction by P. Foner. 464pp. 5⅜ x 8½.
22457-0 Pa. $5.50

LIVING MY LIFE, Emma Goldman. Candid, no holds barred account by foremost American anarchist: her own life, anarchist movement, famous contemporaries, ideas and their impact. Struggles and confrontations in America, plus deportation to U.S.S.R. Shocking inside account of persecution of anarchists under Lenin. 13 plates. Total of 944pp. 5⅜ x 8½.
22543-7, 22544-5 Pa., Two-vol. set $11.00

LETTERS AND NOTES ON THE MANNERS, CUSTOMS AND CONDITIONS OF THE NORTH AMERICAN INDIANS, George Catlin. Classic account of life among Plains Indians: ceremonies, hunt, warfare, etc. Dover edition reproduces for first time all original paintings. 312 plates. 572pp. of text. 6⅛ x 9¼.   22118-0, 22119-9 Pa.. Two-vol. set $11.50

THE MAYA AND THEIR NEIGHBORS, edited by Clarence L. Hay, others. Synoptic view of Maya civilization in broadest sense, together with Northern, Southern neighbors. Integrates much background, valuable detail not elsewhere. Prepared by greatest scholars: Kroeber, Morley, Thompson, Spinden, Vaillant, many others. Sometimes called Tozzer Memorial Volume. 60 illustrations, linguistic map. 634pp. 5⅜ x 8½.
23510-6 Pa. $7.50

HANDBOOK OF THE INDIANS OF CALIFORNIA, A. L. Kroeber. Foremost American anthropologist offers complete ethnographic study of each group. Monumental classic. 459 illustrations, maps. 995pp. 5⅜ x 8½.
23368-5 Pa. $10.00

SHAKTI AND SHAKTA, Arthur Avalon. First book to give clear, cohesive analysis of Shakta doctrine, Shakta ritual and Kundalini Shakti (yoga). Important work by one of world's foremost students of Shaktic and Tantric thought. 732pp. 5⅜ x 8½. (Available in U.S. only)
23645-5 Pa. $7.95

AN INTRODUCTION TO THE STUDY OF THE MAYA HIEROGLYPHS, Syvanus Griswold Morley. Classic study by one of the truly great figures in hieroglyph research. Still the best introduction for the student for reading Maya hieroglyphs. New introduction by J. Eric S. Thompson. 117 illustrations. 284pp. 5⅜ x 8½.
23108-9 Pa. $4.00

A STUDY OF MAYA ART, Herbert J. Spinden. Landmark classic interprets Maya symbolism, estimates styles, covers ceramics, architecture, murals, stone carvings as artforms. Still a basic book in area. New introduction by J. Eric Thompson. Over 750 illustrations. 341pp. 8⅜ x 11¼.
21235-1 Pa. $6.95

ART FORMS IN NATURE, Ernst Haeckel. Multitude of strangely beautiful natural forms: Radiolaria, Foraminifera, jellyfishes, fungi, turtles, bats, etc. All 100 plates of the 19th-century evolutionist's *Kunstformen der Natur* (1904). 100pp. 9⅜ x 12¼.
22987-4 Pa. $4.50

CHILDREN: A PICTORIAL ARCHIVE FROM NINETEENTH-CENTURY SOURCES, edited by Carol Belanger Grafton. 242 rare, copyright-free wood engravings for artists and designers. Widest such selection available. All illustrations in line. 119pp. 8⅜ x 11¼.
23694-3 Pa. $3.50

WOMEN: A PICTORIAL ARCHIVE FROM NINETEENTH-CENTURY SOURCES, edited by Jim Harter. 391 copyright-free wood engravings for artists and designers selected from rare periodicals. Most extensive such collection available. All illustrations in line. 128pp. 9 x 12.
23703-6 Pa. $4.50

ARABIC ART IN COLOR, Prisse d'Avennes. From the greatest ornamentalists of all time—50 plates in color, rarely seen outside the Near East, rich in suggestion and stimulus. Includes 4 plates on covers. 46pp. 9⅜ x 12¼.
23658-7 Pa. $6.00

AUTHENTIC ALGERIAN CARPET DESIGNS AND MOTIFS, edited by June Beveridge. Algerian carpets are world famous. Dozens of geometrical motifs are charted on grids, color-coded, for weavers, needleworkers, craftsmen, designers. 53 illustrations plus 4 in color. 48pp. 8¼ x 11. (Available in U.S. only)
23650-1 Pa. $1.75

DICTIONARY OF AMERICAN PORTRAITS, edited by Hayward and Blanche Cirker. 4000 important Americans, earliest times to 1905, mostly in clear line. Politicians, writers, soldiers, scientists, inventors, industrialists, Indians, Blacks, women, outlaws, etc. Identificatory information. 756pp. 9¼ x 12¾.
21823-6 Clothbd. $40.00

HOW THE OTHER HALF LIVES, Jacob A. Riis. Journalistic record of filth, degradation, upward drive in New York immigrant slums, shops, around 1900. New edition includes 100 original Riis photos, monuments of early photography. 233pp. 10 x 7⅞.
22012-5 Pa. $6.00

NEW YORK IN THE THIRTIES, Berenice Abbott. Noted photographer's fascinating study of city shows new buildings that have become famous and old sights that have disappeared forever. Insightful commentary. 97 photographs. 97pp. 11⅜ x 10.
22967-X Pa. $5.00

MEN AT WORK, Lewis W. Hine. Famous photographic studies of construction workers, railroad men, factory workers and coal miners. New supplement of 18 photos on Empire State building construction. New introduction by Jonathan L. Doherty. Total of 69 photos. 63pp. 8 x 10¾.
23475-4 Pa. $3.00

DRAWINGS OF WILLIAM BLAKE, William Blake. 92 plates from Book of Job, *Divine Comedy, Paradise Lost,* visionary heads, mythological figures, Laocoon, etc. Selection, introduction, commentary by Sir Geoffrey Keynes. 178pp. 8⅛ x 11. 22303-5 Pa. $4.00

ENGRAVINGS OF HOGARTH, William Hogarth. 101 of Hogarth's greatest works: *Rake's Progress, Harlot's Progress, Illustrations for Hudibras, Before and After, Beer Street and Gin Lane,* many more. Full commentary. 256pp. 11 x 13¾. 22479-1 Pa. $7.95

DAUMIER: 120 GREAT LITHOGRAPHS, Honore Daumier. Wide-ranging collection of lithographs by the greatest caricaturist of the 19th century. Concentrates on eternally popular series on lawyers, on married life, on liberated women, etc. Selection, introduction, and notes on plates by Charles F. Ramus. Total of 158pp. 9⅜ x 12¼. 23512-2 Pa. $5.50

DRAWINGS OF MUCHA, Alphonse Maria Mucha. Work reveals drafts-man of highest caliber: studies for famous posters and paintings, render-ings for book illustrations and ads, etc. 70 works, 9 in color; including 6 items not drawings. Introduction. List of illustrations. 72pp. 9⅜ x 12¼. (Available in U.S. only) 23672-2 Pa. $4.00

GIOVANNI BATTISTA PIRANESI: DRAWINGS IN THE PIERPONT MORGAN LIBRARY, Giovanni Battista Piranesi. For first time ever all of Morgan Library's collection, world's largest. 167 illustrations of rare Piranesi drawings—archeological, architectural, decorative and visionary. Essay, detailed list of drawings, chronology, captions. Edited by Felice Stampfle. 144pp. 9⅜ x 12¼. 23714-1 Pa. $7.50

NEW YORK ETCHINGS (1905-1949), John Sloan. All of important American artist's N.Y. life etchings. 67 works include some of his best art; also lively historical record—Greenwich Village, tenement scenes. Edited by Sloan's widow. Introduction and captions. 79pp. 8⅜ x 11¼. 23651-X Pa. $4.00

CHINESE PAINTING AND CALLIGRAPHY: A PICTORIAL SURVEY, Wan-go Weng. 69 fine examples from John M. Crawford's matchless private collection: landscapes, birds, flowers, human figures, etc., plus calligraphy. Every basic form included: hanging scrolls, handscrolls, album leaves, fans, etc. 109 illustrations. Introduction. Captions. 192pp. 8⅞ x 11¾. 23707-9 Pa. $7.95

DRAWINGS OF REMBRANDT, edited by Seymour Slive. Updated Lipp-mann, Hofstede de Groot edition, with definitive scholarly apparatus. All portraits, biblical sketches, landscapes, nudes, Oriental figures, classical studies, together with selection of work by followers. 550 illustrations. Total of 630pp. 9⅛ x 12¼. 21485-0, 21486-9 Pa., Two-vol. set $15.00

THE DISASTERS OF WAR, Francisco Goya. 83 etchings record horrors of Napoleonic wars in Spain and war in general. Reprint of 1st edition, plus 3 additional plates. Introduction by Philip Hofer. 97pp. 9⅜ x 8¼. 21872-4 Pa. $3.75

HISTORY OF BACTERIOLOGY, William Bulloch. The only comprehensive history of bacteriology from the beginnings through the 19th century. Special emphasis is given to biography-Leeuwenhoek, etc. Brief accounts of 350 bacteriologists form a separate section. No clearer, fuller study, suitable to scientists and general readers, has yet been written. 52 illustrations. 448pp. 5⅝ x 8¼.   23761-3 Pa. $6.50

THE COMPLETE NONSENSE OF EDWARD LEAR, Edward Lear. All nonsense limericks, zany alphabets, Owl and Pussycat, songs, nonsense botany, etc., illustrated by Lear. Total of 321pp. 5⅜ x 8½. (Available in U.S. only)
20167-8 Pa. $3.00

INGENIOUS MATHEMATICAL PROBLEMS AND METHODS, Louis A. Graham. Sophisticated material from Graham *Dial*, applied and pure; stresses solution methods. Logic, number theory, networks, inversions, etc. 237pp. 5⅜ x 8½.   20545-2 Pa. $3.50

BEST MATHEMATICAL PUZZLES OF SAM LOYD, edited by Martin Gardner. Bizarre, original, whimsical puzzles by America's greatest puzzler. From fabulously rare *Cyclopedia*, including famous 14-15 puzzles, the Horse of a Different Color, 115 more. Elementary math. 150 illustrations. 167pp. 5⅜ x 8½.   20498-7 Pa. $2.75

THE BASIS OF COMBINATION IN CHESS, J. du Mont. Easy-to-follow, instructive book on elements of combination play, with chapters on each piece and every powerful combination team—two knights, bishop and knight, rook and bishop, etc. 250 diagrams. 218pp. 5⅜ x 8½. (Available in U.S. only)
23644-7 Pa. $3.50

MODERN CHESS STRATEGY, Ludek Pachman. The use of the queen, the active king, exchanges, pawn play, the center, weak squares, etc. Section on rook alone worth price of the book. Stress on the moderns. Often considered the most important book on strategy. 314pp. 5⅜ x 8½.
20290-9 Pa. $4.50

LASKER'S MANUAL OF CHESS, Dr. Emanuel Lasker. Great world champion offers very thorough coverage of all aspects of chess. Combinations, position play, openings, end game, aesthetics of chess, philosophy of struggle, much more. Filled with analyzed games. 390pp. 5⅜ x 8½.
20640-8 Pa. $5.00

500 MASTER GAMES OF CHESS, S. Tartakower, J. du Mont. Vast collection of great chess games from 1798-1938, with much material nowhere else readily available. Fully annotated, arranged by opening for easier study. 664pp. 5⅜ x 8½.   23208-5 Pa. $7.50

A GUIDE TO CHESS ENDINGS, Dr. Max Euwe, David Hooper. One of the finest modern works on chess endings. Thorough analysis of the most frequently encountered endings by former world champion. 331 examples, each with diagram. 248pp. 5⅜ x 8½.   23332-4 Pa. $3.50

HOLLYWOOD GLAMOUR PORTRAITS, edited by John Kobal. 145 photos capture the stars from 1926-49, the high point in portrait photography. Gable, Harlow, Bogart, Bacall, Hedy Lamarr, Marlene Dietrich, Robert Montgomery, Marlon Brando, Veronica Lake; 94 stars in all. Full background on photographers, technical aspects, much more. Total of 160pp. 8⅜ x 11¼.   23352-9 Pa. $6.00

THE NEW YORK STAGE: FAMOUS PRODUCTIONS IN PHOTO-GRAPHS, edited by Stanley Appelbaum. 148 photographs from Museum of City of New York show 142 plays, 1883-1939. *Peter Pan, The Front Page, Dead End, Our Town,* O'Neill, hundreds of actors and actresses, etc. Full indexes. 154pp. 9½ x 10.   23241-7 Pa. $6.00

MASTERS OF THE DRAMA, John Gassner. Most comprehensive history of the drama, every tradition from Greeks to modern Europe and America, including Orient. Covers 800 dramatists, 2000 plays; biography, plot summaries, criticism, theatre history, etc. 77 illustrations. 890pp. 5⅜ x 8½.
20100-7 Clothbd. $10.00

THE GREAT OPERA STARS IN HISTORIC PHOTOGRAPHS, edited by James Camner. 343 portraits from the 1850s to the 1940s: Tamburini, Mario, Caliapin, Jeritza, Melchior, Melba, Patti, Pinza, Schipa, Caruso, Farrar, Steber, Gobbi, and many more—270 performers in all. Index. 199pp. 8⅜ x 11¼.   23575-0 Pa. $6.50

J. S. BACH, Albert Schweitzer. Great full-length study of Bach, life, background to music, music, by foremost modern scholar. Ernest Newman translation. 650 musical examples. Total of 928pp. 5⅜ x 8½. (Available in U.S. only)   21631-4, 21632-2 Pa., Two-vol. set $10.00

COMPLETE PIANO SONATAS, Ludwig van Beethoven. All sonatas in the fine Schenker edition, with fingering, analytical material. One of best modern editions. Total of 615pp. 9 x 12. (Available in U.S. only)
23134-8, 23135-6 Pa., Two-vol. set $15.00

KEYBOARD MUSIC, J. S. Bach. Bach-Gesellschaft edition. For harpsichord, piano, other keyboard instruments. English Suites, French Suites, Six Partitas, Goldberg Variations, Two-Part Inventions, Three-Part Sinfonias. 312pp. 8⅛ x 11. (Available in U.S. only)   22360-4 Pa. $6.95

FOUR SYMPHONIES IN FULL SCORE, Franz Schubert. Schubert's four most popular symphonies: No. 4 in C Minor ("Tragic"); No. 5 in B-flat Major; No. 8 in B Minor ("Unfinished"); No. 9 in C Major ("Great"). Breitkopf & Hartel edition. Study score. 261pp. 9⅜ x 12¼.
23681-1 Pa. $6.50

THE AUTHENTIC GILBERT & SULLIVAN SONGBOOK, W. S. Gilbert, A. S. Sullivan. Largest selection available; 92 songs, uncut, original keys, in piano rendering approved by Sullivan. Favorites and lesser-known fine numbers. Edited with plot synopses by James Spero. 3 illustrations. 399pp. 9 x 12.   23482-7 Pa. $7.95

HOUSEHOLD STORIES BY THE BROTHERS GRIMM. All the great Grimm stories: "Rumpelstiltskin," "Snow White," "Hansel and Gretel," etc., with 114 illustrations by Walter Crane. 269pp. 5⅜ x 8½.
21080-4 Pa. $3.00

SLEEPING BEAUTY, illustrated by Arthur Rackham. Perhaps the fullest, most delightful version ever, told by C. S. Evans. Rackham's best work. 49 illustrations. 110pp. 7⅞ x 10¾.
22756-1 Pa. $2.50

AMERICAN FAIRY TALES, L. Frank Baum. Young cowboy lassoes Father Time; dummy in Mr. Floman's department store window comes to life; and 10 other fairy tales. 41 illustrations by N. P. Hall, Harry Kennedy, Ike Morgan, and Ralph Gardner. 209pp. 5⅜ x 8½.
23643-9 Pa. $3.00

THE WONDERFUL WIZARD OF OZ, L. Frank Baum. Facsimile in full color of America's finest children's classic. Introduction by Martin Gardner. 143 illustrations by W. W. Denslow. 267pp. 5⅜ x 8½.
20691-2 Pa. $3.50

THE TALE OF PETER RABBIT, Beatrix Potter. The inimitable Peter's terrifying adventure in Mr. McGregor's garden, with all 27 wonderful, full-color Potter illustrations. 55pp. 4¼ x 5½. (Available in U.S. only)
22827-4 Pa. $1.25

THE STORY OF KING ARTHUR AND HIS KNIGHTS, Howard Pyle. Finest children's version of life of King Arthur. 48 illustrations by Pyle. 131pp. 6⅛ x 9¼.
21445-1 Pa. $4.95

CARUSO'S CARICATURES, Enrico Caruso. Great tenor's remarkable caricatures of self, fellow musicians, composers, others. Toscanini, Puccini, Farrar, etc. Impish, cutting, insightful. 473 illustrations. Preface by M. Sisca. 217pp. 8⅜ x 11¼.
23528-9 Pa. $6.95

PERSONAL NARRATIVE OF A PILGRIMAGE TO ALMADINAH AND MECCAH, Richard Burton. Great travel classic by remarkably colorful personality. Burton, disguised as a Moroccan, visited sacred shrines of Islam, narrowly escaping death. Wonderful observations of Islamic life, customs, personalities. 47 illustrations. Total of 959pp. 5⅜ x 8½.
21217-3, 21218-1 Pa., Two-vol. set $12.00

INCIDENTS OF TRAVEL IN YUCATAN, John L. Stephens. Classic (1843) exploration of jungles of Yucatan, looking for evidences of Maya civilization. Travel adventures, Mexican and Indian culture, etc. Total of 669pp. 5⅜ x 8½.
20926-1, 20927-X Pa., Two-vol. set $7.90

AMERICAN LITERARY AUTOGRAPHS FROM WASHINGTON IRVING TO HENRY JAMES, Herbert Cahoon, et al. Letters, poems, manuscripts of Hawthorne, Thoreau, Twain, Alcott, Whitman, 67 other prominent American authors. Reproductions, full transcripts and commentary. Plus checklist of all American Literary Autographs in The Pierpont Morgan Library. Printed on exceptionally high-quality paper. 136 illustrations. 212pp. 9⅛ x 12¼.
23548-3 Pa. $7.95

"OSCAR" OF THE WALDORF'S COOKBOOK, Oscar Tschirky. Famous American chef reveals 3455 recipes that made Waldorf great; cream of French, German, American cooking, in all categories. Full instructions, easy home use. 1896 edition. 907pp. 6⅝ x 9⅜. 20790-0 Clothbd. $15.00

COOKING WITH BEER, Carole Fahy. Beer has as superb an effect on food as wine, and at fraction of cost. Over 250 recipes for appetizers, soups, main dishes, desserts, breads, etc. Index. 144pp. 5⅜ x 8½. (Available in U.S. only) 23661-7 Pa. $2.50

STEWS AND RAGOUTS, Kay Shaw Nelson. This international cookbook offers wide range of 108 recipes perfect for everyday, special occasions, meals-in-themselves, main dishes. Economical, nutritious, easy-to-prepare: goulash, Irish stew, boeuf bourguignon, etc. Index. 134pp. 5⅜ x 8½. 23662-5 Pa. $2.50

DELICIOUS MAIN COURSE DISHES, Marian Tracy. Main courses are the most important part of any meal. These 200 nutritious, economical recipes from around the world make every meal a delight. "I . . . have found it so useful in my own household,"—*N.Y. Times.* Index. 219pp. 5⅜ x 8½. 23664-1 Pa. $3.00

FIVE ACRES AND INDEPENDENCE, Maurice G. Kains. Great back-to-the-land classic explains basics of self-sufficient farming: economics, plants, crops, animals, orchards, soils, land selection, host of other necessary things. Do not confuse with skimpy faddist literature; Kains was one of America's greatest agriculturalists. 95 illustrations. 397pp. 5⅜ x 8½. 20974-1 Pa.$3.95

A PRACTICAL GUIDE FOR THE BEGINNING FARMER, Herbert Jacobs. Basic, extremely useful first book for anyone thinking about moving to the country and starting a farm. Simpler than Kains, with greater emphasis on country living in general. 246pp. 5⅜ x 8½. 23675-7 Pa. $3.50

A GARDEN OF PLEASANT FLOWERS (PARADISI IN SOLE: PARADISUS TERRESTRIS), John Parkinson. Complete, unabridged reprint of first (1629) edition of earliest great English book on gardens and gardening. More than 1000 plants & flowers of Elizabethan, Jacobean garden fully described, most with woodcut illustrations. Botanically very reliable, a "speaking garden" of exceeding charm. 812 illustrations. 628pp. 8½ x 12¼. 23392-8 Clothbd. $25.00

ACKERMANN'S COSTUME PLATES, Rudolph Ackermann. Selection of 96 plates from the *Repository of Arts,* best published source of costume for English fashion during the early 19th century. 12 plates also in color. Captions, glossary and introduction by editor Stella Blum. Total of 120pp. 8⅜ x 11¼. 23690-0 Pa. $4.50

PRINCIPLES OF ORCHESTRATION, Nikolay Rimsky-Korsakov. Great classical orchestrator provides fundamentals of tonal resonance, progression of parts, voice and orchestra, tutti effects, much else in major document. 330pp. of musical excerpts. 489pp. 6½ x 9¼. 21266-1 Pa. $6.00

TRISTAN UND ISOLDE, Richard Wagner. Full orchestral score with complete instrumentation. Do not confuse with piano reduction. Commentary by Felix Mottl, great Wagnerian conductor and scholar. Study score. 655pp. 8⅛ x 11. 22915-7 Pa. $12.50

REQUIEM IN FULL SCORE, Giuseppe Verdi. Immensely popular with choral groups and music lovers. Republication of edition published by C. F. Peters, Leipzig, n. d. German frontmaker in English translation. Glossary. Text in Latin. Study score. 204pp. 9⅜ x 12¼.

23682-X Pa. $6.00

COMPLETE CHAMBER MUSIC FOR STRINGS, Felix Mendelssohn. All of Mendelssohn's chamber music: Octet, 2 Quintets, 6 Quartets, and Four Pieces for String Quartet. (Nothing with piano is included). Complete works edition (1874-7). Study score. 283 pp. 9⅜ x 12¼.

23679-X Pa. $6.95

POPULAR SONGS OF NINETEENTH-CENTURY AMERICA, edited by Richard Jackson. 64 most important songs: "Old Oaken Bucket," "Arkansas Traveler," "Yellow Rose of Texas," etc. Authentic original sheet music, full introduction and commentaries. 290pp. 9 x 12. 23270-0 Pa. $6.00

COLLECTED PIANO WORKS, Scott Joplin. Edited by Vera Brodsky Lawrence. Practically all of Joplin's piano works—rags, two-steps, marches, waltzes, etc., 51 works in all. Extensive introduction by Rudi Blesh. Total of 345pp. 9 x 12. 23106-2 Pa. $14.95

BASIC PRINCIPLES OF CLASSICAL BALLET, Agrippina Vaganova. Great Russian theoretician, teacher explains methods for teaching classical ballet; incorporates best from French, Italian, Russian schools. 118 illustrations. 175pp. 5⅜ x 8½. 22036-2 Pa. $2.50

CHINESE CHARACTERS, L. Wieger. Rich analysis of 2300 characters according to traditional systems into primitives. Historical-semantic analysis to phonetics (Classical Mandarin) and radicals. 820pp. 6⅛ x 9¼.

21321-8 Pa. $10.00

EGYPTIAN LANGUAGE: EASY LESSONS IN EGYPTIAN HIERO-GLYPHICS, E. A. Wallis Budge. Foremost Egyptologist offers Egyptian grammar, explanation of hieroglyphics, many reading texts, dictionary of symbols. 246pp. 5 x 7½. (Available in U.S. only)

21394-3 Clothbd. $7.50

AN ETYMOLOGICAL DICTIONARY OF MODERN ENGLISH, Ernest Weekley. Richest, fullest work, by foremost British lexicographer. Detailed word histories. Inexhaustible. Do not confuse this with Concise Etymological Dictionary, which is abridged. Total of 856pp. 6½ x 9¼.

21873-2, 21874-0 Pa., Two-vol. set $12.00

THE AMERICAN SENATOR, Anthony Trollope. Little known, long unavailable Trollope novel on a grand scale. Here are humorous comment on American vs. English culture, and stunning portrayal of a heroine/villainess. Superb evocation of Victorian village life. 561pp. 5⅜ x 8½.
23801-6 Pa. $6.00

WAS IT MURDER? James Hilton. The author of Lost Horizon and Goodbye, Mr. Chips wrote one detective novel (under a pen-name) which was quickly forgotten and virtually lost, even at the height of Hilton's fame. This edition brings it back—a finely crafted public school puzzle resplendent with Hilton's stylish atmosphere. A thoroughly English thriller by the creator of Shangri-la. 252pp. 5⅜ x 8. (Available in U.S. only)
23774-5 Pa. $3.00

CENTRAL PARK: A PHOTOGRAPHIC GUIDE, Victor Laredo and Henry Hope Reed. 121 superb photographs show dramatic views of Central Park: Bethesda Fountain, Cleopatra's Needle, Sheep Meadow, the Blockhouse, plus people engaged in many park activities: ice skating, bike riding, etc. Captions by former Curator of Central Park, Henry Hope Reed, provide historical view, changes, etc. Also photos of N.Y. landmarks on park's periphery. 96pp. 8½ x 11.
23750-8 Pa. $4.50

NANTUCKET IN THE NINETEENTH CENTURY, Clay Lancaster. 180 rare photographs, stereographs, maps, drawings and floor plans recreate unique American island society. Authentic scenes of shipwreck, lighthouses, streets, homes are arranged in geographic sequence to provide walking-tour guide to old Nantucket existing today. Introduction, captions. 160pp. 8⅞ x 11¾.
23747-8 Pa. $6.95

STONE AND MAN: A PHOTOGRAPHIC EXPLORATION, Andreas Feininger. 106 photographs by Life photographer Feininger portray man's deep passion for stone through the ages. Stonehenge-like megaliths, fortified towns, sculpted marble and crumbling tenements show textures, beauties, fascination. 128pp. 9¼ x 10¾.
23756-7 Pa. $5.95

CIRCLES, A MATHEMATICAL VIEW, D. Pedoe. Fundamental aspects of college geometry, non-Euclidean geometry, and other branches of mathematics: representing circle by point. Poincare model, isoperimetric property, etc. Stimulating recreational reading. 66 figures. 96pp. 5⅝ x 8¼.
63698-4 Pa. $2.75

THE DISCOVERY OF NEPTUNE, Morton Grosser. Dramatic scientific history of the investigations leading up to the actual discovery of the eighth planet of our solar system. Lucid, well-researched book by well-known historian of science. 172pp. 5⅜ x 8½.
23726-5 Pa. $3.00

THE DEVIL'S DICTIONARY. Ambrose Bierce. Barbed, bitter, brilliant witticisms in the form of a dictionary. Best, most ferocious satire America has produced. 145pp. 5⅜ x 8½.
20487-1 Pa. $2.00

THE ANATOMY OF THE HORSE, George Stubbs. Often considered the great masterpiece of animal anatomy. Full reproduction of 1766 edition, plus prospectus; original text and modernized text. 36 plates. Introduction by Eleanor Garvey. 121pp. 11 x 14¾.   23402-9 Pa. $6.00

BRIDGMAN'S LIFE DRAWING, George B. Bridgman. More than 500 illustrative drawings and text teach you to abstract the body into its major masses, use light and shade, proportion; as well as specific areas of anatomy, of which Bridgman is master. 192pp. 6½ x 9¼. (Available in U.S. only)
22710-3 Pa. $3.00

ART NOUVEAU DESIGNS IN COLOR, Alphonse Mucha, Maurice Verneuil, Georges Auriol. Full-color reproduction of *Combinaisons ornementales* (c. 1900) by Art Nouveau masters. Floral, animal, geometric, interlacings, swashes—borders, frames, spots—all incredibly beautiful. 60 plates, hundreds of designs. 9⅜ x 8-1/16.   22885-1 Pa. $4.00

FULL-COLOR FLORAL DESIGNS IN THE ART NOUVEAU STYLE, E. A. Seguy. 166 motifs, on 40 plates, from *Les fleurs et leurs applications decoratives* (1902): borders, circular designs, repeats, allovers, "spots." All in authentic Art Nouveau colors. 48pp. 9⅜ x 12¼.
23439-8 Pa. $5.00

A DIDEROT PICTORIAL ENCYCLOPEDIA OF TRADES AND IN-DUSTRY, edited by Charles C. Gillispie. 485 most interesting plates from the great French Encyclopedia of the 18th century show hundreds of working figures, artifacts, process, land and cityscapes; glassmaking, paper-making, metal extraction, construction, weaving, making furniture, clothing, wigs, dozens of other activities. Plates fully explained. 920pp. 9 x 12.
22284-5, 22285-3 Clothbd., Two-vol. set $40.00

HANDBOOK OF EARLY ADVERTISING ART, Clarence P. Hornung. Largest collection of copyright-free early and antique advertising art ever compiled. Over 6,000 illustrations, from Franklin's time to the 1890's for special effects, novelty. Valuable source, almost inexhaustible.
Pictorial Volume. Agriculture, the zodiac, animals, autos, birds, Christmas, fire engines, flowers, trees, musical instruments, ships, games and sports, much more. Arranged by subject matter and use. 237 plates. 288pp. 9 x 12.
20122-8 Clothbd. $13.50

Typographical Volume. Roman and Gothic faces ranging from 10 point to 300 point, "Barnum," German and Old English faces, script, logotypes, scrolls and flourishes, 1115 ornamental initials, 67 complete alphabets, more. 310 plates. 320pp. 9 x 12.   20123-6 Clothbd. $15.00

CALLIGRAPHY (CALLIGRAPHIA LATINA), J. G. Schwandner. High point of 18th-century ornamental calligraphy. Very ornate initials, scrolls, borders, cherubs, birds, lettered examples. 172pp. 9 x 13.
20475-8 Pa. $6.00

THE COMPLETE WOODCUTS OF ALBRECHT DURER, edited by Dr. W. Kurth. 346 in all: "Old Testament," "St. Jerome," "Passion," "Life of Virgin," Apocalypse," many others. Introduction by Campbell Dodgson. 285pp. 8½ x 12¼. 21097-9 Pa. $7.50

DRAWINGS OF ALBRECHT DURER, edited by Heinrich Wolfflin. 81 plates show development from youth to full style. Many favorites; many new. Introduction by Alfred Werner. 96pp. 8⅛ x 11. 22352-3 Pa. $5.00

THE HUMAN FIGURE, Albrecht Dürer. Experiments in various techniques—stereometric, progressive proportional, and others. Also life studies that rank among finest ever done. Complete reprinting of *Dresden Sketch-book*. 170 plates. 355pp. 8⅜ x 11¼. 21042-1 Pa. $7.95

OF THE JUST SHAPING OF LETTERS, Albrecht Dürer. Renaissance artist explains design of Roman majuscules by geometry, also Gothic lower and capitals. Grolier Club edition. 43pp. 7⅞ x 10¾ 21306-4 Pa. $8.00

TEN BOOKS ON ARCHITECTURE, Vitruvius. The most important book ever written on architecture. Early Roman aesthetics, technology, classical orders, site selection, all other aspects. Stands behind everything since. Morgan translation. 331pp. 5⅜ x 8½. 20645-9 Pa. $4.00

THE FOUR BOOKS OF ARCHITECTURE, Andrea Palladio. 16th-century classic responsible for Palladian movement and style. Covers classical architectural remains, Renaissance revivals, classical orders, etc. 1738 Ware English edition. Introduction by A. Placzek. 216 plates. 110pp. of text. 9½ x 12¾. 21308-0 Pa. $8.95

HORIZONS, Norman Bel Geddes. Great industrialist stage designer, "father of streamlining," on application of aesthetics to transportation, amusement, architecture, etc. 1932 prophetic account; function, theory, specific projects. 222 illustrations. 312pp. 7⅞ x 10¾. 23514-9 Pa. $6.95

FRANK LLOYD WRIGHT'S FALLINGWATER, Donald Hoffmann. Full, illustrated story of conception and building of Wright's masterwork at Bear Run, Pa. 100 photographs of site, construction, and details of completed structure. 112pp. 9¼ x 10. 23671-4 Pa. $5.50

THE ELEMENTS OF DRAWING, John Ruskin. Timeless classic by great Viltorian; starts with basic ideas, works through more difficult. Many practical exercises. 48 illustrations. Introduction by Lawrence Campbell. 228pp. 5⅜ x 8½. 22730-8 Pa. $2.75

GIST OF ART, John Sloan. Greatest modern American teacher, Art Students League, offers innumerable hints, instructions, guided comments to help you in painting. Not a formal course. 46 illustrations. Introduction by Helen Sloan. 200pp. 5⅜ x 8½. 23435-5 Pa. $4.00

THE CURVES OF LIFE, Theodore A. Cook. Examination of shells, leaves, horns, human body, art, etc., in *"the* classic reference on how the golden ratio applies to spirals and helices in nature . . . ."—Martin Gardner. 426 illustrations. Total of 512pp. 5⅜ x 8½.   23701-X Pa. $5.95

AN ILLUSTRATED FLORA OF THE NORTHERN UNITED STATES AND CANADA, Nathaniel L. Britton, Addison Brown. Encyclopedic work covers 4666 species, ferns on up. Everything. Full botanical information, illustration for each. This earlier edition is preferred by many to more recent revisions. 1913 edition. Over 4000 illustrations, total of 2087pp. 6⅛ x 9¼.   22642-5, 22643-3, 22644-1 Pa., Three-vol. set $24.00

MANUAL OF THE GRASSES OF THE UNITED STATES, A. S. Hitchcock, U.S. Dept. of Agriculture. The basic study of American grasses, both indigenous and escapes, cultivated and wild. Over 1400 species. Full descriptions, information. Over 1100 maps, illustrations. Total of 1051pp. 5⅜ x 8½.   22717-0, 22718-9 Pa., Two-vol. set $15.00

THE CACTACEAE,, Nathaniel L. Britton, John N. Rose. Exhaustive, definitive. Every cactus in the world. Full botanical descriptions. Thorough statement of nomenclatures, habitat, detailed finding keys. The one book needed by every cactus enthusiast. Over 1275 illustrations. Total of 1080pp. 8 x 10¼.   21191-6, 21192-4 Clothbd., Two-vol. set $35.00

AMERICAN MEDICINAL PLANTS, Charles F. Millspaugh. Full descriptions, 180 plants covered: history; physical description; methods of preparation with all chemical constituents extracted; all claimed curative or adverse effects. 180 full-page plates. Classification table. 804pp. 6½ x 9¼.
23034-1 Pa. $10.00

A MODERN HERBAL, Margaret Grieve. Much the fullest, most exact, most useful compilation of herbal material. Gigantic alphabetical encyclopedia, from aconite to zedoary, gives botanical information, medical properties, folklore, economic uses, and much else. Indispensable to serious reader. 161 illustrations. 888pp. 6½ x 9¼. (Available in U.S. only)
22798-7, 22799-5 Pa., Two-vol. set $12.00

THE HERBAL or GENERAL HISTORY OF PLANTS, John Gerard. The 1633 edition revised and enlarged by Thomas Johnson. Containing almost 2850 plant descriptions and 2705 superb illustrations, Gerard's *Herbal* is a monumental work, the book all modern English herbals are derived from, the one herbal every serious enthusiast should have in its entirety. Original editions are worth perhaps $750. 1678pp. 8½ x 12¼.
23147-X Clothbd. $50.00

MANUAL OF THE TREES OF NORTH AMERICA, Charles S. Sargent. The basic survey of every native tree and tree-like shrub, 717 species in all. Extremely full descriptions, information on habitat, growth, locales, economics, etc. Necessary to every serious tree lover. Over 100 finding keys. 783 illustrations. Total of 986pp. 5⅜ x 8½.
20277-1, 20278-X Pa., Two-vol. set $10.00

THE DEPRESSION YEARS AS PHOTOGRAPHED BY ARTHUR ROTH-STEIN, Arthur Rothstein. First collection devoted entirely to the work of outstanding 1930s photographer: famous dust storm photo, ragged children, unemployed, etc. 120 photographs. Captions. 119pp. 9¼ x 10¾.
23590-4 Pa. $5.00

CAMERA WORK: A PICTORIAL GUIDE, Alfred Stieglitz. All 559 illustrations and plates from the most important periodical in the history of art photography, *Camera Work* (1903-17). Presented four to a page, reduced in size but still clear, in strict chronological order, with complete captions. Three indexes. Glossary. Bibliography. 176pp. 8⅜ x 11¼.
23591-2 Pa. $6.95

ALVIN LANGDON COBURN, PHOTOGRAPHER, Alvin L. Coburn. Revealing autobiography by one of greatest photographers of 20th century gives insider's version of Photo-Secession, plus comments on his own work. 77 photographs by Coburn. Edited by Helmut and Alison Gernsheim. 160pp. 8⅛ x 11.
23685-4 Pa. $6.00

NEW YORK IN THE FORTIES, Andreas Feininger. 162 brilliant photographs by the well-known photographer, formerly with *Life* magazine, show commuters, shoppers, Times Square at night, Harlem nightclub, Lower East Side, etc. Introduction and full captions by John von Hartz. 181pp. 9¼ x 10¾.
23585-8 Pa. $6.00

GREAT NEWS PHOTOS AND THE STORIES BEHIND THEM, John Faber. Dramatic volume of 140 great news photos, 1855 through 1976, and revealing stories behind them, with both historical and technical information. Hindenburg disaster, shooting of Oswald, nomination of Jimmy Carter, etc. 160pp. 8¼ x 11.
23667-6 Pa. $5.00

THE ART OF THE CINEMATOGRAPHER, Leonard Maltin. Survey of American cinematography history and anecdotal interviews with 5 masters—Arthur Miller, Hal Mohr, Hal Rosson, Lucien Ballard, and Conrad Hall. Very large selection of behind-the-scenes production photos. 105 photographs. Filmographies. Index. Originally *Behind the Camera.* 144pp. 8¼ x 11.
23686-2 Pa. $5.00

DESIGNS FOR THE THREE-CORNERED HAT (LE TRICORNE), Pablo Picasso. 32 fabulously rare drawings—including 31 color illustrations of costumes and accessories—for 1919 production of famous ballet. Edited by Parmenia Migel, who has written new introduction. 48pp. 9⅜ x 12¼.
(Available in U.S. only)
23709-5 Pa. $5.00

NOTES OF A FILM DIRECTOR, Sergei Eisenstein. Greatest Russian filmmaker explains montage, making of *Alexander Nevsky,* aesthetics; comments on self, associates, great rivals (Chaplin), similar material. 78 illustrations. 240pp. 5⅜ x 8½.
22392-2 Pa. $4.50

THE EARLY WORK OF AUBREY BEARDSLEY, Aubrey Beardsley. 157 plates, 2 in color: *Manon Lescaut, Madame Bovary, Morte Darthur, Salome,* other. Introduction by H. Marillier. 182pp. 8⅛ x 11. 21816-3 Pa. $4.50

THE LATER WORK OF AUBREY BEARDSLEY, Aubrey Beardsley. Exotic masterpieces of full maturity: *Venus and Tannhauser, Lysistrata, Rape of the Lock, Volpone,* Savoy material, etc. 174 plates, 2 in color. 186pp. 8⅛ x 11. 21817-1 Pa. $4.50

THOMAS NAST'S CHRISTMAS DRAWINGS, Thomas Nast. Almost all Christmas drawings by creator of image of Santa Claus as we know it, and one of America's foremost illustrators and political cartoonists. 66 illustrations. 3 illustrations in color on covers. 96pp. 8⅜ x 11¼. 23660-9 Pa. $3.50

THE DORÉ ILLUSTRATIONS FOR DANTE'S DIVINE COMEDY, Gustave Doré. All 135 plates from Inferno, Purgatory, Paradise; fantastic tortures, infernal landscapes, celestial wonders. Each plate with appropriate (translated) verses. 141pp. 9 x 12. 23231-X Pa. $4.50

DORÉ'S ILLUSTRATIONS FOR RABELAIS, Gustave Doré. 252 striking illustrations of *Gargantua and Pantagruel* books by foremost 19th-century illustrator. Including 60 plates, 192 delightful smaller illustrations. 153pp. 9 x 12. 23656-0 Pa. $5.00

LONDON: A PILGRIMAGE, Gustave Doré, Blanchard Jerrold. Squalor, riches, misery, beauty of mid-Victorian metropolis; 55 wonderful plates, 125 other illustrations, full social, cultural text by Jerrold. 191pp. of text. 9⅜ x 12¼. 22306-X Pa. $6.00

THE RIME OF THE ANCIENT MARINER, Gustave Doré, S. T. Coleridge. Dore's finest work, 34 plates capture moods, subtleties of poem. Full text. Introduction by Millicent Rose. 77pp. 9¼ x 12. 22305-1 Pa. $3.50

THE DORE BIBLE ILLUSTRATIONS, Gustave Doré. All wonderful, detailed plates: Adam and Eve, Flood, Babylon, Life of Jesus, etc. Brief King James text with each plate. Introduction by Millicent Rose. 241 plates. 241pp. 9 x 12. 23004-X Pa. $6.00

THE COMPLETE ENGRAVINGS, ETCHINGS AND DRYPOINTS OF ALBRECHT DURER. "Knight, Death and Devil"; "Melencolia," and more—all Dürer's known works in all three media, including 6 works formerly attributed to him. 120 plates. 235pp. 8⅜ x 11¼. 22851-7 Pa. $6.50

MAXIMILIAN'S TRIUMPHAL ARCH, Albrecht Dürer and others. Incredible monument of woodcut art: 8 foot high elaborate arch—heraldic figures, humans, battle scenes, fantastic elements—that you can assemble yourself. Printed on one side, layout for assembly. 143pp. 11 x 16. 21451-6 Pa. $5.00

TONE POEMS, SERIES II: TILL EULENSPIEGELS LUSTIGE STREICHE, ALSO SPRACH ZARATHUSTRA, AND EIN HELDEN-LEBEN, Richard Strauss. Three important orchestral works, including very popular *Till Eulenspiegel's Marry Pranks,* reproduced in full score from original editions. Study score. 315pp. 9⅜ x 12¼. (Available in U.S. only)
23755-9 Pa. $7.50

TONE POEMS, SERIES I: DON JUAN, TOD UND VERKLARUNG AND DON QUIXOTE, Richard Strauss. Three of the most often performed and recorded works in entire orchestral repertoire, reproduced in full score from original editions. Study score. 286pp. 9⅜ x 12¼. (Available in U.S. only)
23754-0 Pa. $7.50

11 LATE STRING QUARTETS, Franz Joseph Haydn. The form which Haydn defined and "brought to perfection." (*Grove's*). 11 string quartets in complete score, his last and his best. The first in a projected series of the complete Haydn string quartets. Reliable modern Eulenberg edition, otherwise difficult to obtain. 320pp. 8⅜ x 11¼. (Available in U.S. only)
23753-2 Pa. $6.95

FOURTH, FIFTH AND SIXTH SYMPHONIES IN FULL SCORE, Peter Ilyitch Tchaikovsky. Complete orchestral scores of Symphony No. 4 in F Minor, Op. 36; Symphony No. 5 in E Minor, Op. 64; Symphony No. 6 in B Minor, "Pathetique," Op. 74. Bretikopf & Hartel eds. Study score. 480pp. 9⅜ x 12¼.
23861-X Pa. $10.95

THE MARRIAGE OF FIGARO: COMPLETE SCORE, Wolfgang A. Mozart. Finest comic opera ever written. Full score, not to be confused with piano renderings. Peters edition. Study score. 448pp. 9⅜ x 12¼. (Available in U.S. only)
23751-6 Pa. $11.95

"IMAGE" ON THE ART AND EVOLUTION OF THE FILM, edited by Marshall Deutelbaum. Pioneering book brings together for first time 38 groundbreaking articles on early silent films from *Image* and 263 illustrations newly shot from rare prints in the collection of the International Museum of Photography. A landmark work. Index. 256pp. 8¼ x 11.
23777-X Pa. $8.95

AROUND-THE-WORLD COOKY BOOK, Lois Lintner Sumption and Marguerite Lintner Ashbrook. 373 cooky and frosting recipes from 28 countries (America, Austria, China, Russia, Italy, etc.) include Viennese kisses, rice wafers, London strips, lady fingers, hony, sugar spice, maple cookies, etc. Clear instructions. All tested. 38 drawings. 182pp. 5⅜ x 8.
23802-4 Pa. $2.50

THE ART NOUVEAU STYLE, edited by Roberta Waddell. 579 rare photographs, not available elsewhere, of works in jewelry, metalwork, glass, ceramics, textiles, architecture and furniture by 175 artists—Mucha, Seguy, Lalique, Tiffany, Gaudin, Hohlwein, Saarinen, and many others. 288pp. 8⅜ x 11¼.
23515-7 Pa. $6.95

UNCLE SILAS, J. Sheridan LeFanu. Victorian Gothic mystery novel, considered by many best of period, even better than Collins or Dickens. Wonderful psychological terror. Introduction by Frederick Shroyer. 436pp. 5⅜ x 8½.
21715-9 Pa. $6.00

JURGEN, James Branch Cabell. The great erotic fantasy of the 1920's that delighted thousands, shocked thousands more. Full final text, Lane edition with 13 plates by Frank Pape. 346pp. 5⅜ x 8½.
23507-6 Pa. $4.50

THE CLAVERINGS, Anthony Trollope. Major novel, chronicling aspects of British Victorian society, personalities. Reprint of Cornhill serialization, 16 plates by M. Edwards; first reprint of full text. Introduction by Norman Donaldson. 412pp. 5⅜ x 8½.
23464-9 Pa. $5.00

KEPT IN THE DARK, Anthony Trollope. Unusual short novel about Victorian morality and abnormal psychology by the great English author. Probably the first American publication. Frontispiece by Sir John Millais. 92pp. 6½ x 9¼.
23609-9 Pa. $2.50

RALPH THE HEIR, Anthony Trollope. Forgotten tale of illegitimacy, inheritance. Master novel of Trollope's later years. Victorian country estates, clubs, Parliament, fox hunting, world of fully realized characters. Reprint of 1871 edition. 12 illustrations by F. A. Faser. 434pp. of text. 5⅜ x 8½.
23642-0 Pa. $5.00

YEKL and THE IMPORTED BRIDEGROOM AND OTHER STORIES OF THE NEW YORK GHETTO, Abraham Cahan. Film *Hester Street* based on *Yekl* (1896). Novel, other stories among first about Jewish immigrants of N.Y.'s East Side. Highly praised by W. D. Howells—Cahan "a new star of realism." New introduction by Bernard C. Richards. 240pp. 5⅜ x 8½.
22427-9 Pa. $3.50

THE HIGH PLACE, James Branch Cabell. Great fantasy writer's enchanting comedy of disenchantment set in 18th-century France. Considered by some critics to be even better than his famous *Jurgen*. 10 illustrations and numerous vignettes by noted fantasy artist Frank C. Pape. 320pp. 5⅜ x 8½.
23670-6 Pa. $4.00

ALICE'S ADVENTURES UNDER GROUND, Lewis Carroll. Facsimile of ms. Carroll gave Alice Liddell in 1864. Different in many ways from final Alice. Handlettered, illustrated by Carroll. Introduction by Martin Gardner. 128pp. 5⅜ x 8½.
21482-6 Pa. $2.00

FAVORITE ANDREW LANG FAIRY TALE BOOKS IN MANY COLORS, Andrew Lang. The four Lang favorites in a boxed set—the complete *Red, Green, Yellow* and *Blue* Fairy Books. 164 stories; 439 illustrations by Lancelot Speed, Henry Ford and G. P. Jacomb Hood. Total of about 1500pp. 5⅜ x 8½.
23407-X Boxed set, Pa. $14.95

THE STANDARD BOOK OF QUILT MAKING AND COLLECTING, Marguerite Ickis. Full information, full-sized patterns for making 46 traditional quilts, also 150 other patterns. Quilted cloths, lame, satin quilts, etc. 483 illustrations. 273pp. 6⅞ x 9⅝. 20582-7 Pa. $4.95

ENCYCLOPEDIA OF VICTORIAN NEEDLEWORK, S. Caulfield, Blanche Saward. Simply inexhaustible gigantic alphabetical coverage of every traditional needlecraft—stitches, materials, methods, tools, types of work; definitions, many projects to be made. 1200 illustrations; double-columned text. 697pp. 8⅛ x 11. 22800-2, 22801-0 Pa., Two-vol. set $12.00

MECHANICK EXERCISES ON THE WHOLE ART OF PRINTING, Joseph Moxon. First complete book (1683-4) ever written about typography, a compendium of everything known about printing at the latter part of 17th century. Reprint of 2nd (1962) Oxford Univ. Press edition. 74 illustrations. Total of 550pp. 6⅛ x 9¼. 23617-X Pa. $7.95

PAPERMAKING, Dard Hunter. Definitive book on the subject by the foremost authority in the field. Chapters dealing with every aspect of history of craft in every part of the world. Over 320 illustrations. 2nd, revised and enlarged (1947) edition. 672pp. 5⅜ x 8½. 23619-6 Pa. $7.95

THE ART DECO STYLE, edited by Theodore Menten. Furniture, jewelry, metalwork, ceramics, fabrics, lighting fixtures, interior decors, exteriors, graphics from pure French sources. Best sampling around. Over 400 photographs. 183pp. 8⅜ x 11¼. 22824-X Pa. $6.00